Why No Beethoven?

Why No Beethoven?

Humphrey Lyttelton

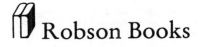 Robson Books

FIRST PUBLISHED IN GREAT BRITAIN IN 1984 BY
ROBSON BOOKS LTD., BOLSOVER HOUSE, 5-6
CLIPSTONE STREET, LONDON W1P 7EB. COPYRIGHT
© 1984 HUMPHREY LYTTELTON.

British Library Cataloguing in Publication Data

Lyttelton, Humphrey
  Why no Beethoven?
  1. Jazz music—Anecdotes, facetiae, satire
  I. Title
  785.42   ML3561
  ISBN 0-86051-262-2

Printed in Great Britain by
Biddles Ltd., Guildford

Contents

The Bands

POLAND, 1976
>Bruce Turner, alto, clarinet
>Kathy Stobart, tenor, baritone
>Mick Pyne, piano
>Harvey Weston, bass
>Tony Mann, drums

MIDDLE EAST, 1979
>Bruce Turner, alto, clarinet
>John Barnes, baritone, clarinet
>Roy Williams, trombone
>Mick Pyne, piano
>Dave Green, bass
>Alan Jackson, drums

MIDDLE EAST, 1982
>Same as 1979, except that Mike Paxton replaced Alan Jackson on drums

Preface

In 1974, I started keeping a day-to-day diary. Its purpose was not to consign innermost thoughts and dark secrets to posterity, but to help me remember people, places and incidents. It's from the parts of that journal which cover my band tours of Poland and the Middle East that this book is taken, with bits added here and there.

A further *aide-mémoire* has been provided by tape-recordings which Alan Jackson and Mick Pyne made at odd—sometimes very odd—moments, and I am grateful for the loan of them. I thank also the British Council and all who sail in her for providing the tours for me to write about.

H.L.

Thursday, 21 October 1976, Warsaw

Left London Airport at 9.35 on a Russian Ilyushin belonging to the official Polish Lot Airline—a vast plane with room for my legs! Back in the Fifties there were two pastimes which had a certain glamour and sexiness about them—doing television and travelling by air. Then the accountants moved in and each turned into a hassle. Most commercial aeroplanes nowadays remind me of the trucks on North African railways that boasted accommodation for forty persons or eight horses.

In today's plane, the welcome spaciousness is offset by dreadfully pompous Eastern European muzak. Come to think of it, all airline muzak is dire, a conspiracy between the companies and otherwise unemployable musical arrangers to persuade the nervous that anything—take-off, turbulence, travel-sickness, the possibility of engine failure, collision, hi-jacking or sabotage—is preferable to remaining imprisoned on the ground with that horribly jolly music.

We are met at Warsaw Airport by a young member of the Polish Jazz Festival organization. He introduces himself as Mark, though it later transpires that he spells it Marek. A pleasant-looking blond with a ready grin, though there is something curiously lop-sided about his jaw-line. In him we have our first encounter with the Polish sense of humour, quite similar to the English in its self-deprecating and faintly surrealistic leanings. He says that for the next five days he will be our mother and father.

From the airport we are driven to the Europejski Hotel

which is alleged to be extremely comfortable. Judging by the vast modern foyer it is a typical American-style 'international' hotel with rooms that are low in personality but high in modern conveniences. Unfortunately, the foyer is all we see of it, since they know nothing of our booking. All cock-ups begin at Calais! Mark walks us across the road to the Bristol Hotel, where they are expecting us. Mick Pyne, our piano player, among whose hobbies is the collecting of books, recorded speeches and other archive material relating to World War II, remembers with some excitement that it was here that Hitler had his headquarters in 1939 at the culmination of the Polish campaign. It now looks ripe for demolition, some parts of the façade having jumped the gun and fallen off spontaneously. The interior is redolent with 'atmosphere'—the focal point of the huge foyer is a vast, ornate lift, an open, wrought-iron cage similar to the one in which Katharine Hepburn made her majestic descent in *Suddenly Last Summer*. It takes us up to rooms which are indescribably run-down. The rock-hard beds lean to starboard or sag amidships, the walls are cracked, peeling and stained with damp, and in the bathrooms the fittings are encrusted with dirt and populated by tiny brown beetles that come up through the plug-holes. Spirits, often depressed on arrival at a new place, are at rock-bottom as we get ready to go to the Kongress Hall for rehearsal.

The Polish Jazz Festival has grown from small beginnings in the Fifties to become one of the largest in Europe, with bands from both sides of the Iron Curtain assembling during the five days. Hitler failed to suppress the underground jazz movements in the occupied countries during the war, and similar attempts by the post-war Communist regimes to ban the 'decadent product of an artistically bankrupt capitalist system' have had to give way in the face of the fanatical dedication and enthusiasm of generations of young fans. (I remember giving an informal lecture in my office to some members of the visiting Red Army Orchestra in the late Fifties. They showed polite interest in the urban folk-jazz of such proletarian heroes as George Lewis and Bunk Johnson, but perked up mightily when I came to Benny Goodman and Glenn Miller.) Once the official ban on jazz was lifted in 1955, Poland caught up with fifty-odd years of jazz history in one mad sprint. Everything from basic Dixieland to extreme avant-garde now flourishes.

An East German band is rehearsing incomprehensible avant-garde music when we arrive at the Kongress Hall, but we soon get to run through our four numbers.

Mark says there is no car or bus to take us back to the hotel so we buy tickets at a nearby newspaper kiosk and go by bus. We have each been given a wad of Polish zlotys to cover expenses. Before we left England, we received enigmatic advice to take with us the full visitors' allowance of twenty-five pounds sterling. I can't see why—it looks as if our expense allowance is going to be more than ample. And it's easier to pronounce 'zlotys' (we must learn to say 'zwotties') than to find out what they represent in English money. Mark is vague when we enquire but steers us away from the exchange bureau at the airport where the official rate is 32 Zl to the pound. He is surprisingly unenthusiastic about the rate at the hotel desk, which is up to 53 Zl to the pound. So we stow our English pounds away and forget about them.

They say that the food at the Bristol Hotel is the best in Warsaw, so we eat in the massive, Thirties-style dining-room. I am normally allergic to waiters who hover. Ours, an olive-skinned fatty who would not have been out of place in an Edward G. Robinson gangster movie, practically alights in my lap. The food, in the shashlik and schnitzel category, is ordinary but not bad, but a half-bottle of alleged Bordeaux at the equivalent of £8 makes the eyes water both metaphorically and literally. As he serves coffee the waiter, with whom we have hitherto conversed in a mixture of pidgin English and sign language, bends over us conspiratorially and says, in perfect English, 'Surely you have some money to change—pounds or dollars?' 'Yes,' we mumble, matching his furtiveness. 'Fold them in your napkin,' he whispers before gliding away. After some debate we decide to risk all—theft, fraud, arrest, deportation—and follow his instructions. When he has cleared away the coffee cups and departed, we peek rather nervously into the folds of the napkin. Hey presto! Twenty-five English pounds have turned into three thousand, seven hundred and fifty zlotys, at the rate of 150 Zl to the pound. No wonder Mark was reluctant to see us change money through the usual channels!

Back at the Kongress Hall we wait our turn to go on. The East German avant-garde band looks even scruffier and hairier than at rehearsal. Have they actually dressed *down* for the gig itself? Their act is oddly schizoid. They present obscure, introverted music with all the noisy heartiness of a trad band. They get an ovation from the packed house—we are told that there will be 5,000 people in on every one of the five nights, and ticket prices are soaring on the black market. I have chosen three originals of mine plus Duke Ellington's 'Creole Love Call', and we do 'St Louis Blues' for an encore, which the audience demands from us as they did from the far-out German band. Backstage, I run into Willis Conover, the jazz Voice of America, whom I hadn't expected to see. He's an old chum from our US tour in '59, though I find his rather owlish erudition daunting. That fishy stare through the thick glasses could convince an Einstein that he was talking bilge. He tells me that he has just finished a book of personal reminiscences of H. P. Lovecraft. I daren't let on that I don't know who H. P. Lovecraft is—I must look him up in *Hot Discography* when I get home.

My impression after one concert is that, in Poland, pretentious avant-garde jazz has a firm hold, with the uncommunicative, freaky image much in evidence. But straightforward, toe-tapping music manifestly cheers the audience up.

Friday, 22 October 1976, Warsaw
Ham and eggs at 10 a.m. in the breakfast room, which turns out to be the very room from which Hitler emerged on to the balcony to review his triumphant troops. As we stand on it looking down into the broad street below, by coincidence a small parade marches by led by a military band. We resist the urge to give it the benedictory Hitler salute. An eerie experience.

After breakfast we wander out towards the city centre, loaded with zlotys and bent upon shedding some of them. It is clearly easier for the foreigner to acquire them than to spend them. Every few yards we are accosted by quite respectable-looking citizens offering to exchange them, often at an even better rate than that given by last night's waiter. Having been

12

primed with the dangers and penalties inherent in the strict currency laws, we find it odd and disturbing that all this hustling goes on under the noses of the police. We are told later that the authorities are ambivalent about it—it is against the law but, on the other hand, it brings a lot of very welcome Western currency into the country.

It soon transpires that Warsaw is not the place for a shopping spree. Even Kathy Stobart, who could write a directory of the department stores of the world and whose appearance on homebound aircraft, festooned with clanking plastic shopping bags, gives her fellow-travellers serious concern about the feasibility of take-off, finds little joy in the Warsaw equivalent of Marks and Sparks. Bruce Turner, a staunch communist, is the only one of us not dismayed by the general shoddiness of the goods, but he pitches his sights low. All he wants to buy is a Chinese-style, Mao Tse-tung jacket. Why he should expect to find one in Warsaw I don't know, but in the event he fails, walking out muttering 'They won't sell me a Mao jacket, they won't sell me a Mao jacket.'

Bruce's eccentricity is legendary in the jazz world. A lot of it, no doubt, is a sedulously-acquired cloak to conceal a natural diffidence. But in most of the extraordinary utterances there is a genuinely original flair for, and enjoyment of, words. In Turnerese, the American saxophonist Lucky Thompson becomes Fortunate Thompson, and the series of recordings featuring Buck Clayton Jam Sessions are spoonerized into the Jack Clayton Bum Sessions. A now-forgotten American movie comedian called Hugh Herbert instilled in him years ago the habit of saying everything twice. From early comics and Billy Bunter stories came the ludicrously archaic phrases—'Some fun I'd say' (abbreviated now to 'Some fun, some fun'), 'This is the life for a chap, life for a chap' or 'Gosh, thanks'—which take the place of more humdrum clichés. Sometimes apparent gibberish turns out to be a conventional phrase mangled in deliberate, usually rhythmic, mispronunciation. Fans or promoters who invite him out after a concert are often bewildered to have their invitation declined in what sounds like a mixture of Swahili and scat-singing. 'Gudder gudder be-DERLY, gudder gudder be-DERLY.' It is left to us to explain, after he has hurried away to his hotel room, that what he said was 'Got to go to bed early'. In Sweden, years ago, we all ate at a cafeteria. In the queue to the check-out, someone told him that it is proper in Sweden to say 'Tak' (Thank you) as you pay your bill. 'Never!' was Bruce's first response, but his informant insisted. By the time he reached the desk he had devised a way of avoiding the—to him—embarrassing abruptness of the monosyllable. As he handed over his money, he leant forward and, in his customary half-whisper, said to the astonished lady cashier, 'Tak for the meal, Dad, tak for the meal, tak tiddly ack tack, meal meal.'

Not one zloty do I part with on this first visit to the shops. It's not just that there is nothing attractive to buy; one is also deprived of the mild interest to be found in picking things up and looking at them. The goods are not accessible as in Western shops but are stacked on shelves behind the assistants' counter, so you have to point at whatever you want. With such a laborious procedure there's little scope for choice. There is also a lot of queueing, especially in the meat shops where supplies are low. Mark tells us that shoppers queue at the butcher's in front of empty counters, waiting for new supplies to come in—and when they do, there is often a free fight to get to the front. We pass one small shop where fists are indeed flying on the pavement outside, but it turns out to be selling fur coats. When I call on the man from the British Council— our sponsors for this tour—he tells me that leather and amber are the only two commodities likely to attract the visitor from the West.

We are on late tonight, so I go back to the hotel for a sleep and dinner. It was back in 1956, when I was on tour with Sidney Bechet and simultaneously trying to write and send off story material for the *Daily Mail* comic strip, *Flook*, that I first practised the relaxation exercises in Dr Grantly Dick-Read's book about painless childbirth, and acquired the knack of sending myself to sleep—and waking myself up—at will. The book (or some article that I've read since) suggested that it helps if you lie spread-eagled on the bed and concentrate on the sensation of falling. I go one better, imagining myself to be King Kong, in the final scene from the eponymous movie, falling from the Empire State Building *and still twenty feet from the pavement*. It works a treat. Apart from providing easy

14

cat-naps, it accounts for the fact that I have driven an average of forty thousand miles a year for twenty years or more without once, touch wood, having fallen asleep at the wheel. A rapidly-induced ten minutes' kip in a lay-by gives one an hour-and-a-half of driving free from the numb head and the swivelling eyes.

At dinner, I discover that Haddock Old Polish Style is identical to the family favourite which we call Eggy Fish at home—haddock or cod poached in milk and served in a thick duvet of parsley sauce with hard boiled eggs. I've eaten it for years, and never realized that it is an old Polish speciality.

At 11.15 p.m. we go on stage at a small students' club which is one of the several fringe venues at the Festival. It's pretty full when we start our one-hour set, and fills up even more when the concert ends over at the Kongress Hall and insatiable fans stream across to us. We get a fine reception, then become involved in an argument backstage with Mark, who tells us that tonight we are expected to stay on and 'make a jam session' with some of the other musicians taking part. I try to explain to him that jam-sessions are born, not made, and that in view of the music emanating from the stage while we speak, we have little in common with the other much more modern band on the show. I say that it would be like holding a conversation in two different languages without an interpreter. 'But,' he cries, 'that will make interesting music!' 'Not for me!' I say, packing up my trumpet and striding out of the building. Indignant exits are invariably ill-fated. A cloudburst is in progress outside and there is no sign of a taxi, so I have to go back in. However, it is now established that we make no jam-session, so an amiable atmosphere is restored, at least until it becomes clear that no transport has been arranged to get us back to the hotel. Mark commandeers a punter as he leaves the club, offers him 50 Zl to take us. He agrees, but won't take the money, saying 'I am a jazz fan.'

Saturday 23 October 1976, Warsaw
They serve a delicious brand of coddled egg in a special glass in Hitler's old antechamber—just the thing after a night of vodka and ill temper. Two Swedish promoters come to the

hotel this morning to discuss the possibility of a tour of the Swedish Folk Parks by the band next year. One of them is called Ake Forsberg, a name that could have come from one of those Forties swing band personnels which my father used to get me to read out to him whenever he felt in need of entertainment. He hated swing music but loved the personnels and selected reading from *Hot Discography*. One of his favourites was Sam Donohue's Navy Band in 1945. By the time I had got through Conrad Gozzo, Tasso Harris, Dick Le Fave, Tak Takvorian, Joe Aglora, Al Horish, Barney Spieler and Buz Sithens he would be mopping his eyes. He is the only person I ever knew who, at the end of a movie, would not make a dash for the cinema exit once the credits began rolling. He stayed in his seat, glued to the screen, enjoying the rich variety of American names which, he insisted, must have derived from anagrams concocted around the font.

As always on tour, there is a lot of sitting around—waiting for radio interviewers, newspaper people, promoters, coach drivers and so on. The foyer of the Bristol Hotel offers plenty of entertainment of a faintly sleazy but intriguing kind. We are fascinated by the activities of one small, ferrety man who seems to be permanently attached to the place. He is perpetually on the go, disappearing out into the street, hurrying back in, circulating among the guests as they check in and out and, occasionally, seizing a new arrival confidentially by the elbow and steering him or her into the ornate lift. Throughout the day his movements become less and less coordinated and late at night he is literally staggering, but it doesn't seem to interfere with what are clearly entrepreneural operations. We think we have nailed him as the local 'fixer'—cameras, girls, currency, you name it. It was he, we reckon, who rang Mick Pyne's room at random in the middle of last night and asked thickly, 'You like man?'

I should have asked him to get me the small notebook that I need for keeping account of expenses, etc. At a nearby stationer's I queued in a line which snaked round three sides of the shop before reaching a solitary assistant, for whom I pointed at what seemed to be the only notebook in the place. I am something of a notebook fetishist, often cherishing the feel of a well-designed book so much that I'm reluctant to start writing in it. This one's a measly thing.

Mark had arranged to take us to the old town at 3 p.m. but he arrives at the hotel an hour late and looking ashen, having had what he described cryptically as a 'life crash'. Without explaining further he goes off again, so we make our way to the old town on our own. Almost completely destroyed during the war, this part of the city has been rebuilt exactly as it was, using the original material salvaged from the rubble. The result is staggering, especially surveyed from the centre of the huge square. Tall, narrow buildings, loftily gabled and subtly varied in colour, seem to huddle protectively, shoulder to shoulder, round the central space, and the whole scene has the hazy, pinkish patina of an old painting under the evening sun. On this rather hurried trip we are here, not to sightsee, but to off-load our embarrassment of zlotys. On the man from the British Council's advice I go for amber, which is on display in the windows of poky little shops in great toffee-like lumps. As one would expect from fossilized resin it *feels* rather like toffee, too—warm, slightly gummy and comforting to handle rather than icily 'precious'. The made-up necklaces remind me of the strings of homemade crystallized coffee sugar on which I ruined my teeth as a boy. The one I choose for Jill costs 2000 Zl, achieving at a stroke the redistribution of otherwise useless currency and a splendid bargain in waiter-money.

Our evening concert is in another students' hall further out of town, a barn-like room with poor acoustics. Several bands are crammed into one communal dressing-room and one of them, called the Vistula River Jazz Band (trad jazz names are the same the world over), sets up in a corner and plays at us relentlessly all night, except for a brief moment of respite when they are actually on stage playing for the public. It is this tendency to play with manic enthusiasm on every possible occasion that distinguishes the amateur jazz musician from the professional, often to the public detriment of the latter, who are regarded as snooty and unfriendly. I can remember travelling by train with George Webb's Dixielanders to a gig in the border town of Hawick, and playing non-stop throughout the journey. When I got out of the carriage my top lip looked as if it was harbouring a burgeoning spring onion, and Wally Fawkes was so musically spent that he left his clarinet under the seat in the compartment. When next thought of, it was far away in Edinburgh and was retrieved from the return train only just in time for the show.

I think the urge to blow whenever opportunity arose came from a mixture of exuberance and optimism. In those innocent days we believed, in the face of all available evidence, that in the very next session we would stop the spinning earth in its tracks. And if we could bring that ecstatic moment forward by striking up on the train, so much the better. Happily, some vestige of that youthful expectation remains through life. But behind it there forms the more realistic ambition just to do one's best and to conserve energy and inspiration for the main event.

During our set (well received) I am somewhat startled by the sudden appearance in the wings of a tramp, long-haired and wispy-bearded, who waves and beams at me as if he knows me well. And indeed he does—it turns out to be Barrett Deems, who was neatly crew-cut when he was over with Louis Armstrong in 1956, but who now looks like Jimmy Durante with a Rasputin hair-do. He and Buddy Tate are over for the Festival with Benny Goodman, and have decided to pay us a surprise visit. Despite the Vistula River Jazz Band we have a good chat in the band room. Buddy says that he endures some ribbing from other musicians because he seems to know someone in every town, city or country that he visits. This time, he told them, 'I'm sure I'm not gonna know anybody in Warsaw'—but when they all trooped out of the airport, somebody walked straight up to him and said 'You know, Humphrey's in town.'

Sunday 24 October 1976, Warsaw
A beautiful sunny day with a clear sky and all the buildings standing out with that razor-edged definition that late autumn sunshine bestows. We go again to the old square which looks marvellous, as busy and animated as a Breughel townscape. Nothing of the dour, Eastern European servile state here. Indeed, the almost tangible spirit of Warsaw is of a robust and often humorous independence.

Mark is sufficiently recovered from shock to divulge that his

18

'life crash' involved leaving his small leather bag containing around 32,000 Zl of box office 'take' in the taxi that took him home on Friday night. He has made all the routine enquiries but never had any hope of seeing it again. He reckons it will take him eighteen months to pay it back. We are not materially affected, but the incident spreads despondency and some remorse among members of the band who have been rather too quick to take him to task for every lapse or breakdown in organization.

There are many jobs within the field of entertainment promotion which are inspiring, creative and rewarding, but acting as the temporary mother and father of a touring jazz band is not one of them. It calls for the combined talents of a lion-tamer, guide-dog, psychiatrist, mind-reader, bodyguard and miracle-worker. The best I ever knew was Duggie Tobutt who looked after visiting American musicians on behalf of the Harold Davison Agency. His secret was that he loved it, and he had it reduced to a fine art. As soon as the band coach arrived at its destination, Duggie would heave his burly but invariably dapper form upright and address his distinguished and stellar charges with the words, 'Now, hear this . . .' All the details for the gig, overnight stay and departure next day would then follow concisely and nothing was ever said twice. With his bald head, well-padded shoulders and ever twinkling, sceptical eyes, he looked the epitome of the 'wide boy', but there wasn't a phoney or snide bone in his body. He was no judge of jazz. Often he would come across backstage when some jazz giant of irrefutable eminence was playing and ask me, 'What d'you think, then—is he any good?'

To Duggie, genius was no excuse or even explanation for unprofessional conduct or bad time-keeping. In Cambridge once, two shaggy student devotees of the profound and eccentric pianist Thelonious Monk managed to get into the Students' Union to hear the master rehearse for a TV show, only to find that after a perfunctory sound-check he had walked out of the building and disappeared. Disappointed, they asked Duggie Tobutt, 'Will Mr Monk be coming back?' and were visibly shocked by the blunt answer, 'How should I know? When you're dealing with Thelonious Monk, you're dealing with an idiot'. Louis, Basie, Duke—possibly Monk, too—all loved him and specifically asked for him on their tours. It was after he had left his prescribed desk-job—he had heart trouble—and returned to the road that he collapsed and died in the manager's office at Batley Variety Club, where Louis was playing.

Mark has neither the talent nor the aspiration to be a Duggie Tobutt—it's the amateur/professional dichotomy once again. He will no doubt say goodbye to us at the end of this tour reinforced in his belief that musicians are a moody and temperamental lot. He may well feel that the grumbles and grouses are poor repayment for his constant equanimity and good humour. But in his job, niceness is not the top priority. Indeed, Duggie Tobutt's popularity proved that in on-duty movements one can be blunt, dictatorial and sometimes positively rude so long as the coach always turns up on time, hotel arrangements are smooth and reliable, and backstage privacy and requirements are safeguarded. It is from this sense of security that all else flows.

This afternoon at two o'clock we assemble to go by coach, with several other bands, to Lodz or, as the Poles have it, Woodge. There is a Hungarian group, a Polish trad band who will back the American trumpeter Wallace Davenport, an American-led avant-garde band, and us. Summoned by Mark, we troop out of the hotel to see, standing outside, the oldest bus ever seen outside a museum. 'Ha ha ha!' we all cry. 'For a moment we thought that old wreck was our band-coach.' 'It is,' says Mark. It's obvious at a glance that there is not room for all the musicians, let alone instruments that include three double-basses and several drum-kits. Wallace Davenport is offered a lift in a private car and gratefully accepts. After many years on the road with Lionel Hampton and a recent severe illness, he has recently returned to take life more easily in his native city of New Orleans. So what is he doing here in Warsaw? His chronic look of deep gloom suggests that he is asking himself the same question.

Since no alternative transport arrives (being a Sunday, there's no one at Festival HQ to cope), we all squeeze into the old banger, which appears to have solid tyres, slack springs, ill-fitting windows and no heating. There is snow about and a wind keen enough to slice onions. Mutiny, as well as frost, is in the air. But it's little use grumbling on these occasions. No amount of stomping about proclaiming that one is a sensitive artiste and swearing like a navvy is going to produce a substitute coach at this late hour, so there is nothing for it but to withdraw tortoise-like into the overcoat and try to induce a state of torpor. 'Oscar Peterson wouldn't put up with this,' somebody says, 'he'd walk straight off the tour.' 'So would I if I had his money,' is my answer as I disappear into my cocoon.

It's a measure of the efficiency of our valiant bus that it takes four freezing and jolting hours to cover the eighty-two miles to Lodz, through dull, homogeneous farmland that offers little diversion. Even the one or two amateur ornithologists among us are doomed to boredom, with nothing to spot but the occasional hooded crow. Handsome birds with their grey velvet doublets, but when you've seen one . . . It's almost dark when we reach Lodz, so we get no more than an impression of a long-drawn-out industrial city. The Filharmonia sounds like a smart hall, but venerable turns out to be the word . . . a bit like Birmingham Town Hall but without the chronic smell of leaking gas. Disasters and discomforts on tour never come singly but breed off themselves. Because the journey took so long, there is too little time to eat before the show. This doesn't prevent the whole cast from trooping across the road to a smart modern hotel for a meal. Smart modern hotels work on the principle that no one would go there unless they had not only money but infinite leisure, so most of us are still clamouring for attention when the concert is due to start. The promoter from the Filharmonia runs in on the verge of heart-failure, but the Hungarian band that is due to open is still unfed and refuses to budge.

Having at least had our starters, we do the British thing and volunteer to open the show instead. The audience is cheerful and enthusiastic, and having got our set out of the way we can listen to some of the other music. Wallace Davenport is a fine player, though his true forte is as a section leader. Modern big band arrangements, such as he played with Lionel Hampton, make such physical and tonal demands on a trumpeter that much of the warmth and intimacy required of a jazz improvisor is lost. This was not always the case—in the mid-Thirties, musicians such as Max Kaminsky, Johnny Best, Pee Wee

Erwin and even Harry James were able to handle the trumpet chores in the big bands of Tommy Dorsey, Artie Shaw and Benny Goodman and at the same time retain their individuality in small groups. Nowadays, players who habitually play first or second trumpet parts spend most of their time playing in the high register at shattering volume. ('It was so loud,' says Jack Sheldon of playing in the lower reaches of Stan Kenton's five-piece trumpet section, 'you didn't have to play the music—it didn't make any difference!') The funny thing is that, in 1938, Benny Goodman's Orchestra caused riots in theatres across America playing arrangements in which the trumpeters worked within the natural range of the instrument and nobody had to go puce in the face. It's all relative, as the man said.

I have a chat with Wallace after his set. Without prompting, he harks back to the occasion in 1967 when the Hampton band went on strike over one of my compositions. Lionel Hampton heard us play a piece called 'Blues in Bolero' at a Jazz Expo concert at which he topped the bill. In his usual excitable way (with Hamp, hysteria is never far below the surface), he grabbed me as I came off stage. 'Hey, Humphrey, bring that blues number down to Ronnie Scott's in the morning—I'm gonna play it on TV.' I thought the whole thing was highly improbable, but I had the piece copied out and duly reported at Ronnie's in the morning. The band was already rehearsing for their BBC-TV show, so I sat in the shadows enjoying the music and little bothered that they seemed to have the programme set without my contribution. The last number they rehearsed was Hamp's theme tune, 'Flyin' Home', during which he led a visibly reluctant band off the stand for a parade round the room. As he passed me, waving vibraphone mallets in the air and braying in ecstasy, he seemed totally carried away. Then he spotted me in the gloom. 'Did you bring that number, have you got that tune? We'll do it next!' His enthusiasm, alas, was not shared by the rest of the band. The piece has a drum introduction in *bolero* rhythm, and his drummer couldn't make it. 'I can't do what your guy does,' he kept saying to me, and I accepted it as a well-deserved compliment to Spike Wells, who was working with me at the time. Hamp looked at me as if expecting me to take charge and run the band through it, a job for which, in Lester Young parlance, I had 'no eyes'. Fortunately, the matter was resolved when the whole band, led by Wallace Davenport, got up without a word and made for the bar, indicating that the rehearsal was over.

I have always assumed that, like me, they instantly put the matter behind them and gave it no further thought. But tonight, Wallace Davenport goes to some lengths to explain that the action was no reflection on myself or my tune, but that having rehearsed numbers that they *knew* all morning, they were in no mood to learn something completely new. I urge him to believe that I would have done the same myself and bear no grudge. His insistence on making amends for the trivial incident distracts me from asking him whether it is really true that, playing for a private boat party on Lake Potomac, Lionel lashed the band into such a frenzy on 'Flyin' Home' that the saxophone section unquestioningly obeyed his exhortations and jumped into the lake, still blowing the compelling riffs. My guess is that the story is about as reliable as the one about Buddy Bolden being heard across Lake Ponchartrain on a clear night. On the other hand, I can testify, having worked with Hamp on stage, that he has a remarkably low frenzy threshold. A few well-timed off-beats from the drums and he's in vertical take-off.

For a while we listen with mounting disbelief to the avantgarde band. Its leader is a bearded American pianist called Michael who has the flowing grey locks and passive, otherworldly look of a love-generation Jesus out of his time. In the line of duty as a jazz presenter on radio, I have listened to a lot of 'free' jazz. To say that I 'understand' it would be both untrue and fatuous. Intrinsic in the term 'free improvisation' is a procedure whereby rules are applied, decisions are made, directions are taken spontaneously rather than in accordance with a pre-ordained plan involving keys, regular metres and 'tempo'. There is no way in which the listener can 'understand' it in the way that he or she recognizes a neat turn of phrase or a subtle variation of harmony in conventional jazz improvisation. One might as usefully peer into an abstract painting in the hope of recognizing a chair, a human face or a vase of flowers.

This is not to say that the listener has no reference points to help distinguish between genuine creativity and charlatanism. Such requirements as stylistic integrity, momentum, dynamic shape and emotional content still apply when the more specific rules and conventions are removed. Through these the experienced (and open-minded) listener can perceive the genuineness or phoniness of a performance. After hearing Archie Shepp's band at Ronnie Scott's Club in the late Sixties I reeled out into the street convinced that it was at least genuine, if only because nobody could possibly keep a joke, a hoax or a con-trick going with such intensity for so long! It was a negative and somewhat frivolous judgement, but it does underline the point that it's through the senses rather than the intellectual understanding that one should expect to receive the initial message of 'free jazz'. Come to think of it, that's the way that most people get the message from any sort of jazz. The trouble with Michael and his team is that their music is *too* easy to understand. Behind the avant-garde posturing, conventional and quite banal chords and rhythms can be spotted lurking and smirking. But not, apparently, by the audience, who lap it all up.

After the concert, it transpires that Michael has arranged to take his sensitive artistes back to Warsaw in a hired Mercedes. I come under intensive pressure to do the same, but I resist. A little healthy stoicism is good for the soul—and works wonders for the wallet. So, soon after ten o'clock we re-embark on the refugee wagon, piling on the overcoats and settling down in the now more generous space into separate, mute mounds of long-suffering. The Hungarian band are more resilient. In the coach's archaic layout, they have seats in the front which face, and are raised above, the rest of us. From this natural stage they decide to launch an impromptu concert of Hungarian folksong, belting out a succession of songs all of which reach a predictable accelerating climax with frenetic hand-clapping and shouts of 'Oi!' I'm ashamed to say that the response among the British contingent is to nestle, like startled hamsters, further into the protective overcoats. The leader of the Hungarians is a young man with frizzy hair and the manic look of Tom Baker's 'Doctor Who'. After a while he hops across to me and, peering into the recesses of my overcoat, shouts: 'Hello . . . these are very old folk-musics from our country. Are you interested of them?' 'Very,' I call back, nestling furiously.

When the Polish band joins in with a couple of their own songs, the scenario acquires a certain inevitability. Doctor Who suddenly claps his hands for silence and announces: 'And now, some singings from the English party!' From each mound of overcoat a balloon emerges bearing the words: 'Oh, God!' The shouts of encouragement become so insistent that I foresee an international 'incident'. Suddenly Harvey Weston, who is our bass-player for the tour, emerges from his cocoon and, with startling verve, launches into 'My old man said follow the van . . .' Harvey might be said to be of studious rather than extrovert appearance, so there's clearly an element of self-sacrifice in his sudden entry into the fray. Encouraged by it, we gradually surface and join in, while the Hungarians listen in awe.

'Let's all go down the Strand', 'Two lovely black eyes,' 'Don't 'ave any more, Mrs Moore'—they follow each other with a vigour born of desperation. During 'Mrs Moore', the only one of which I know the words throughout, Doctor Who hops across and interrupts me. 'You know, these folk-musics are very interesting for us—from what part of England do they come?' 'From the old city of London,' I shout back, and off he goes to impart the information to his compatriots. The four-hour journey seems to take no time at all. As we disembark at our hotel, Doctor Who says, 'When I get home, I will try and arrange that you come to Hungary.' 'That will be nice,' I say, 'we've never played in Hungary.' 'Not to play,' he cries. 'To sing!'

Monday, 25 October 1976, Warsaw

This morning, the foyer of the Bristol Hotel is suddenly invaded by what appears to be an entire tribe of peasants having, like out-of-towners everywhere, a look of bewilderment tempered by confidence in their numbers. There must be four generations represented, and from the oldest to the youngest they have the same powerful, proud, bottom-heavy faces of hewn stone that suggest that they would be more at home on horseback, fur-clad and scanning the plains, than perched on sofas and armchairs in a hotel foyer. Wherever they come from, it is clearly a society in which authority is invested in age and seniority. It's uncomfortable to compare the demeanour of these elders—strong, composed and formidable—with the anxious, defensive look of so many old people back home. Not all—my own upper-class grandparents remained figures of awe and authority until the day they died, and the steel-working and coal-mining communities of South Wales and the North are still dominated by the older generation in domestic affairs. It's in the large and ever-increasing urban area in the middle where loneliness is endemic, that we seem to have gone badly wrong.

At 11 o'clock, a sleeker coach arrives at the hotel to take us to Crakow for our last concert. Over snacks in a road-house en route, a furious row breaks out between Bruce Turner and some members of the band who are less than enchanted with the alleged drabness and material backwardness of Poland, and Warsaw in particular. You can always tell when Bruce is angry: he only says things once. As always, I sit on the sidelines, only occasionally stirring the pot to keep it simmering. With some justification, Bruce accuses them of having a tourist's view of the place, says they should get around and visit people in their homes to find out how they live and what they think. Not an easy thing to do on a busy tour, and I'm not sure that if Bruce carried it out he would get the answers that, as a communist and a Stalinist to boot, he tends to take for granted. My own distinct impression, acquired admittedly by doing no more than sniff the air, is that the Poles think little of the present Russian-dominated regime.

Underneath the drabness, the regimentation and the queue-ing, there's a powerful sense of nationalism and independence, expressed freely now in anti-Russian and anti-government jokes, but one day likely to blow up into another Hungary. There's something distinctly out-of-joint and schizoid about a society in which the citizenry queue for food in the shadow of vast new inter-continental hotels. In the post-war years the British earned the reputation of being queue-happy, but we are a disorganized rabble compared with the Poles. En route for Lodz two days ago, we had a pee-stop at the roadside copse.

We spread out amongst the trees—all except the Polish band, who queued patiently to pee against the same tree.

It's a smooth but boring journey to Crakow. The hearts of the hedonistically-inclined are uplifted when we are signed into a smart American-style hotel in which we can wash, brush up and relax until we return to Warsaw late tonight. We are still heavily loaded with zlotys which we must get rid of before going through customs tomorrow. There is a free hour in which we can visit the shops, so it's a near thing. Crakow seems a more prosperous and sophisticated city than either Warsaw or Lodz, and there are smart shops in which I contrive to buy three fine leather or suede bags, all for less than £4 in waiter-money. I think the heavy leather shoulder-bag which I earmark for myself is really a shooting-bag, but it will be useful for carrying around contracts, VAT invoice books, cheque-book, car documents, and all the other stuff that one has to take to gigs in the streamlined nineteen-seventies.

Going straight to the concert-hall from the shops, I find that the audience is already assembling in the huge foyer. Can't attract anyone's attention at the stage-door, which is locked, so I have to go in through the front, breaking my lifelong rule not to clap eyes on an audience before a show. This has nothing to do with aloofness or show-biz mumbo-jumbo, but for the more down-to-earth reason that it scares me to death. Tonight is a case in point—by the time I have blundered through the hordes of predominantly youthful strangers, trying to find the way through to the back, I am convinced that we are in for an indifferent, if not hostile, reception. As a result, I am clammy with nerves before our set, which is the last one before the interval. We walk on to a warm ovation and a sea of smiles and at the end could cheerfully have done three or four encores.

After us, the show goes on till midnight, so we go back to the hotel for an end-of-term meal. Much better food than at the similarly-rated Bristol Hotel in Warsaw. In a burst of confidentiality, Mark tells me that he has only recently been released from a spell in prison for political activity. His family is both dissident and aristocratic, an unpopular combination. In the course of one interrogation, his inquisitor pointed at the telephone on the desk and asked, 'What is that?' When Mark laughed incredulously at the pointless question, the man seized the handset and smashed it across his face, fracturing his jaw and knocking out several teeth. The episode explains Mark's occasional lapses in concentration and also the lack of symmetry in his jaw-line which we noticed when we first saw him at the airport.

After the meal, we heap all our remaining zlotys in the middle of the table. In their own right they constitute a lavish tip. Recycled by the waiters into dollars or pounds over lunch tomorrow, they will reap a small fortune. We embus for Warsaw soon after midnight, arriving back at the Bristol at about 5 a.m. with time for an hour's rest before being picked up for the airport. A few hours later we say farewell to Mark, who is now green with fatigue, and fly home.

Wednesday, 14 November 1979, Turkey

Alarm call at 5.45. Did all the packing last night, so got off at
6.15 for Heathrow. The car is going to have to put up with two
weeks in the long-term car park. Relying on a hire car to turn
up at this hour of the morning is too nerve-racking. The last
one I had turned out to have a regular contract to take a small
girl to school, so I was taken on a round trip of the leafy
avenues of Stanmore with a mute, uniformed nine-year-old in
the back seat while the minutes to check-in time ticked by.

This time there are no hitches, and we take off at around
9 a.m., losing three hours en route and arriving at Istanbul at
3.30. By dropping the name of a British Airways pilot whom we
had met at a party some weeks ago, we manage to get
permission to visit the flight deck in ones and twos. I am there
as we approach Istanbul, so the captain says, 'You might as
well stay here for the landing.' The runway at Istanbul starts at
the very edge of the cliff overlooking the Sea of Marmara, so
it's rather like alighting on a huge static aircraft carrier. The
chat on the flight deck is too terribly nonchalant and Biggles
for words. I don't grasp the technicalities, but as we drift and
wobble towards the slender sliver of tarmac, I take comments
like 'Might it be a good idea if we checked the jolly old
so-and-so . . .' to imply in reality 'Christ! We've forgotten to
check the bloody so-and-so!' and grip the edge of my seat.
'Quite a few bods down there on the beach,' says the skipper in
conversational tones and I assume that he's assessing the
casualties in the event of our falling an inch or two short of the

runway. It's quite an anticlimax when we make a silky landing.

The show tomorrow is in Ankara, so we have to change planes in Istanbul. We are met by a large, red-bearded man in a flat cap who is Clive Gobby, the assistant British Council representative. With him, the first move is made in a game which is to elate or depress us at each stage in the tour. In countries with strict currency controls, there are problems over transferable fees for touring bands, suffice it to say that a deal has been worked out at home and day-to-day subsistence is our only concern. As we arrive in each new country we shall be given expenses in the local currency to pay for our hotels and meals. We have been assured that they will meet all costs and, allowing for invitations to meals or receptions, may well leave us something to spare for shopping. With all the strange, unconvincing-looking paper money, it promises to be every bit as exciting as Monopoly, with similar bonuses and forfeits according to the throw of the dice. Unfortunately, we start with a forfeit—Clive gives us our quota for the two days we shall spend in Istanbul, saying, 'I'm sorry it's a bit tight.' One of my maxims in life is not to worry about set-backs until they happen, and preferably not even then. Others don't share this philosophy, and there is some despondency.

Istanbul Airport, or rather the section of it that handles internal flights, looks like a rural railway branch-line, full of peasant families with innumerable children and cardboard luggage tied up with string. Some have crates of live chickens similarly secured. Turks in transit seem a sombre lot—everyone is in either black, grey or funeral mauve. There doesn't seem to be any such thing as a timetable with internal flights—they wait until there's a plane-load and just send it off. We have a wait of about forty-five minutes before flying on to Ankara.

After another forty-five minutes aloft, we arrive at Ankara. We're met by a bearded young man who introduces himself as Francis Jurksaitis and hurries on to explain that he is, in fact, English. He is the British Council second-in-command, and his first official function is to hand over our expenses for the two nights in Ankara, which he does with a rueful expression and the hope, expressed none too convincingly, that they will cover everything. He also gives us foolscap sheets with our itinerary for the next thirty-six hours. They are perused in stunned silence, then somebody says, 'Christ!'

Ankara is built on a steep rocky hill that rises quite abruptly out of the plain. Even the ugliest cities—and Ankara is one of them—have their moments, and the sight of foot-hills on either side of the road completely encrusted with small, baked-mud houses that perch precariously on every ledge and promontory, is really rather impressive. It's dusk by now, and the hills are bejewelled. The thing that strikes us next, and more forcibly, is the atmosphere, which carries that acrid, penetrating smell of a neighbour's bonfire. Francis explains that this is a well-known characteristic of Ankara, which lies in what amounts to a crater at the top of the hill and sucks back its own exhalation of wood and coal smoke.

We check into the Bulvar Palas Hotel, a rambling old place with its façade missing and a team of what look like extras from a Hollywood gangster movie behind the reception desk. It is not possible to look trustworthy while wearing dark glasses indoors. Incidentally, we are reminded of the volatile state of Turkish politics at this time by the appearance of two heavily-armed soldiers seemingly on guard outside our hotel. They are not for us—apparently some government personage is either here or expected.

We have now been on the go for about twelve hours, but there is time only for a quick shower before the social events of the day start. When you work for the British Council it is on a quasi-diplomatic level, which means that all parties and receptions listed on the itinerary are obligatory. As most of them involve a buffet meal and therefore count as bonus points in the expenses game, we have no complaints. First event this evening is a get-together with top British Council man Jeremy Barnet and his wife Maureen in the lounge of the Bulvar Palas. With them is a Turkish bass-player, Selçuk Sun (pronounced Selchook Soon), who, we are told, is one of the handful of accomplished and knowledgeable jazz musicians that Turkey has so far produced. He is full of excitement at the prospect of a party at his house tomorrow. Don't remember seeing it on the bandcall, which seemed to me to be choc-a-bloc from lunchtime onwards. So I ask innocently, 'When is that?' 'Tomorrow morning,' he cries, 'immediately after your rehearsal!' A nervous glance at the itinerary confirms that a rehearsal is scheduled for 9.30 a.m., followed by drinks at the house of Mr Sun. A quick word with Francis scotches the rehearsal, but we can't disappoint Selçuk. Nor can we prepare for what promises to be a marathon by having an early night, as there is still a reception at the British Ambassador's before today is out.

Taking account of the three hours that we dropped on the long flight from Heathrow to Istanbul it is still twelve hours since my alarm call this morning. What's more, we have had no opportunity to eat since the meal on the plane at lunchtime. So what remains of today has a dream-like quality. The Embassy is a splendid floodlit affair overlooking the town. Sir Derek and Lady Dodson are charming in the face of the dislocation caused by the late arrival of seven musicians all clamouring for food. Being an after-dinner party, there are only nibbles laid on, but an ambassador's wife is as well-equipped to handle such crises as is her husband in less important matters. Soon we are sitting about in groups among the other guests, voraciously devouring platefuls of meatballs and courgettes in batter, washing them down with Buck's Fizz, and desperately trying to keep a hold on the threads of two or three simultaneous conversations.

Sir Derek, a distinguished-looking amalgam of C. Aubrey Smith and Wilfred Hyde White, is soon to retire and seems, in our brief conversation, to have more than half a mind on that blessed moment. I sympathize with him entirely—a deputation from outer-space would be no harder to converse with in the late hours than a group of travel-weary jazz musicians. Dave Green has brought an electric bass on this trip to make the travelling easier and safer—it's a thin, elongated affair that stands on a spike like the conventional bass, which is why it's nicknamed a 'pogo-stick' in the trade. I mention this to Sir Derek when we're talking about the rigours of touring. 'That's funny,' he said, 'I came across that term for the first time the other day. What exactly *is* a pogo-stick?' At 12.30 at night after a day's travelling, loaded to the gills with battered courgettes and Buck's Fizz, one could as easily explain Einstein's Theory of Relativity. Fortunately, the conversation seemed to fizzle out at that point . . .

34

Back at the hotel, we don't retire to bed at once. Dave Green, who announced five hours ago that he was 'shattered' (like most musicians, he has manic-depressive tendencies and his energies ebb and flow), invites us into his room to listen to some cassettes. As amateur archivists, Dave and Mick Pyne vie with each other in the collecting of esoteric material—old books about Scott of the Antarctic, rare Itma broadcasts, the speeches of Neville Chamberlain, broadcasts by long forgotten comics. My stock as a relic of a departed era, already elevated when Dave unearthed a sound recording of me playing the trumpet outside Buckingham Palace on VE Day, went through the roof when I revealed that I was in the crowd at Croydon Airport in 1938 when Chamberlain waved his piece of paper and said 'Peace in our time'. All of which explains, but only just, why we are still in Dave's room at 2.30 a.m., listening to fuzzy, indistinct recordings of Billy Russell and Norman Long, broadcasting comedians from yesteryear.

Thursday, 15 November 1979, Istanbul
This morning, we're all shattered. Disconcertingly, the acrid pall of wood-smoke has penetrated the hotel, and we walk to the breakfast room with handkerchiefs over our faces.

At 10.30 a.m. we are picked up to go to the party at Selçuk's house, somewhere out in the suburbs. There we meet another leading Turkish musician, drummer Erol Pekcan (pronounced Pekjan), who introduces himself to me as 'your Turkish counterpart'. It transpires that he leads a band and presents jazz on radio and TV. Tallish, bald and pear-shaped, he looks like a cuddly version of the sinister actor, Eric Pohlman. We listen to records, talk jazz and drink coffee, tea and, among the more reckless souls, the Turkish drink raki which belongs to the Pernod family and, like Pernod, brings one's forehead out in a not altogether unpleasant cold sweat after a sip or two.

Fortunately, there is no time to embark on a lost week-end, as we are all due for a lunch with the British Council staff and some TV people who are going to film a short session this afternoon. It's in an upstairs private room in a restaurant and is, if we leave a hurried Continental breakfast at the hotel out of account, the first square meal that we've had since the lunch

35

pack on the plane. It disappears before we have time to analyse exactly what it is we're devouring, but bowls of beans and lumps of lamb just about sums it up. Towards the end, the TV people begin to fidget, for we are due at their studios to record a hasty half-hour show in the early afternoon.

'Hasty' implies an altogether too leisurely process. Arriving at a large, barn-like studio, we are urged to unpack the instruments without delay. While drums and bass are set up, I scribble out some routines for five numbers. It seems that there is a recording deadline, which means that already the 'half-hour' has shrunk to twenty minutes while we plan it. As soon as we're ready, we play a few bars for a sound check—no camera rehearsal—and then an agitated producer shouts over the intercom, 'We must start!' In fact, he shouts something indecipherable in Turkish, but Selçuk has come along as interpreter, and he runs down from the gallery aloft to wave us into action. Breathlessly, we play four of the five numbers, in between which I make announcements into whichever camera appears to be paying attention at the time. Then, on a command from above, everybody seems to relax, the camera-men remove their headsets and someone in the studio says, 'That is all.' 'No it isn't,' I say, 'we have one more piece', and I gesture with a forefinger accordingly. There is an exchange of Turkish between the floor and the gallery, then we are told, 'O.K., but quickly!' I am on the point of beating in the final number when Selçuk, who has been running down the stairs to give us the first message in English and has missed the subsequent changes, bursts into the studio and, with a gesture of finality with both arms over his head, cries 'FINISH!'

End of well-intentioned but ill-conceived TV spot. While we pack up, they play back bits of it. The balance is nowhere— pogo-stick bass predominates while the front-line instruments appear to be joining in from outside in the street. The cameras follow the action as if drugged, zooming in blearily on soloists who have either just finished or are about to start. If ever they do alight on someone who is actually blowing, a great out-of-focus torso moves in to blot out the action. Nothing can be done about it, so why worry? There is no time even to discuss it, since we are late for the sound check at the concert hall and must be hustled once again into cars.

Sound checks should be simple, but are usually a hassle. The idea of having the microphones ready when the musicians arrive has never really established itself. One or two of them are always broken, replacements are never to hand. Most sound men, especially those with long hair wearing body-clinging shirts, work on the principle 'Start loud, and get louder'. I have to throw a medium-sized tantrum to bring the dilatory process to an end, so that we can at least have two hours' rest at the hotel before the concert.

The run-up to the concert exerts its usual revitalizing effect. It's a splendid, dignified hall normally used for symphony concerts. There is an air of excitement backstage—and some curiosity, too, since Ankara is less hip in jazz matters than Istanbul. For us, Turkey offers the perfect arena. It has had some contact with jazz over the post-war years, both 'live' and on record. But unlike Britain and Western Europe, it has not been saturated in it. A two-day visit in 1978 revealed that, in some mysterious way, we have acquired a following here so the shows have a special atmosphere of excitement.

Once onstage, I see that Sir Derek and Lady D. have made it, as has the Chinese Ambassador, who is appropriately inscrutable throughout. Other State dignitaries occupy the front rows, and the rest of the hall is packed. In the interval, we are visited by members of the state symphony orchestra, predominantly young musicians with a great interest in jazz. Jeremy Barnet has suggested to me before the concert that, as a diplomatic exercise, it would be popular if I let Selçuk and Erol join us for a number. I've never heard them play, but decide that, since we are on a quasi-diplomatic mission, it's worth taking a chance. They sit in on 'In a Mellotone', and happily turn out to be accomplished musicians with a complete grasp of jazz. So the exercise is enjoyable and, as Jeremy predicted, extremely popular.

After the concert, we're once again pretty hungry, since there was time only for a hurried bowl of soup beforehand. Fortunately, there are two functions scheduled tonight—a reception in the foyer of the concert-hall, with drinks and snacks, followed by a party with buffet supper at Jeremy and Maureen Barnet's house. I talk myself and everyone else into the ground at each. It is well after midnight when we get back to the hotel, and we have a 7 a.m. call in the morning to fly to Istanbul. My father, faced with a prospect of fine but excessive eating (and using an old-fashioned term for 'to diet') used to say, 'Have we not all eternity to bant in?' I feel the same about sleep when encountering new places and people. Anyway, five and a half hours is enough.

Friday, 16 November 1979, Ankara
Our departure from Ankara is precipitate and chaotic. When we ask for our bills at the desk, they are not ready. Francis Jurksaitis is there to do the ritual shouting, which produces all the accounts on one sheet of paper—useless to us since we are settling separately. The heavies behind the desk make a great show of being unhurried and eventually produce bills which are substantially more than the amount negotiated by Francis yesterday. More shouting, eventual success. We are late for the flight, but it waits for us.

At Istanbul, we are met by Clive Gobby who, we discover, takes a somewhat lugubrious view of life. Driving into the city in his car, I tell him that we are glad to leave the polluted atmosphere of Ankara. 'It'll be worse here,' he says, pointing to a great swathe of blue-black smoke on the horizon. It appears that two tankers, Romanian and Greek, have recently collided in the Bosphorus, and the former has been ablaze for two days, sending up a pall of smoke which, Colin judges, should engulf the Sheraton Hotel with the wind in its present position. We are staying at the Sheraton. When we get there, we find that the cloud misses it by half a mile or so. Some of the band travelling in another car arrive pale and shaken. Seeing a crowd peering over the sea wall by the harbour, their driver stopped to investigate. On the rocks below the wall, a dead sailor rocked gently on the tide, stiff with rigor mortis.

Spirits rise when we find that, by doing a short forty-five minute spot in a bar at the hotel after our concert tonight, we get our hotel accommodation free. Clive leans on them, and they throw in Continental breakfast as well. Even so, our expenses are uncomfortably tight, so for the afternoon meal it's round to an inexpensive café that Clive recommends. Musicians are adept at extracting the maximum nourishment from the minimum outlay. Peasant soups full of chunks of meat and vegetables are always a good bet. Here, kebabs with mountains of rice and salad on the side commend themselves. The meat is a bit scrawny, but there's loads of ballast. Halfway through the meal, Dave Green bites into an innocent-looking chilli and turns such an interesting shade of mottled red that I have to capture the moment with a quick caricature on a table napkin. Am spotted by our waiter, who brings up another napkin and points at himself, asking for the same treatment. His colleagues follow suit, dumping paper in front of me and striking macho poses that somehow miss the point of the exercise. When the rest of the band leave for the hotel and a much-needed rest, I'm still there like Toulouse-Lautrec, working away. I wouldn't mind if they hadn't then presented me with my bill in full. I'm sure Lautrec got a discount.

Our concert this evening is in a cinema over the way from the hotel. The San Cinema holds nine hundred, and is completely sold out. We do one set from 7 to 8.30, since there is some sort of ethnic stage show afterwards. We share the backstage area with berobed men with huge beards and towering hats and buxom ladies in harem attire. Language and musical differences represent a culture gap that's hard to bridge, so our intercourse goes little further than stately bows as we pass each other in the gloom.

The concert is an enormous success, which is more than can be said for the Tommy Tucker exercise at the Sheraton afterwards. There the audience consists of the sort of international bar-flies that infest expensive hotels everywhere— rich, blasé and ineffably smooth. After the San Cinema, which had all the robust atmosphere of a market-place, it's dreary stuff. But it's soon over.

Saturday, 17 November 1979, Istanbul
No need for an alarm clock in Istanbul. Even seven or eight floors above street level, the dawn chorus of car-horns is impressive. In the middle distance out to sea, the Romanian tanker puts on a non-stop show, belching black smoke with undiminishing vigour and occasionally erupting with an

explosive flash of orange flame. They expect it to keep it up for a fortnight.

Yesterday Mr Alper Chaglayan rang me at the hotel and arranged to take me out to lunch today. His brother Ata runs the Chaglayan Kebab House in Hendon, a local haunt of ours and one of the few restaurants of its kind to make the *Good Food Guide*. Ata is a huge, genial man who addresses all his customers, male or female, as 'my love' and has something of the unsymmetrical, awry and eccentrically-bulging look of an over-worked easy chair. As I await Alper in the Sheraton foyer at noon, I wonder if I will recognize him. I worry unduly. The man who comes in, looking round the foyer expectantly, has Ata's generous build and height, although the camel-hair coat, dark glasses and generally square-cut look indicate that working for a multi-national industry in Istanbul brings more earthly rewards than selling shish kebab in Hendon.

His wife Aysel is waiting in a large Mercedes outside, and we glide off to one of the much-acclaimed fish restaurants on the shores of the Bosphorus in the picturesque outskirts of town. Warnings have been broadcast about the danger of eating seafood from the Bosphorus while the crisis over the burning tanker is on, but Alper cheerfully shrugs them off—as do most of the locals, judging from the brisk business along the coast. The 'Middle East' weather so envied by those we left behind has not yet materialized, but it's warm and sunny enough to sit outside the Kosen restaurant, overlooking a pretty harbour, and eat delicious fresh fish, preceded by the ubiquitous *mese* (Turkish hors d'oeuvres of endless variety). The price to pay for idyllic alfresco eating is persistent importuning from gypsy fortune-tellers, children selling flowers, scrofulous alley-cats and beggars of all ages. Alper rewards them all except the cats, and chats with several as if they were old friends.

Afterwards we go shopping and I spend some English money on a fine leather jacket for less than £45. It has been a heavy day for poor Aysel, who speaks no English and has a bad cold, but delightful and relaxing for me. In fact, it has been a good day for all, as Erol came down from Ankara and took some of the others sightseeing. With the end of the Turkish leg in sight, it transpires that there will be some Monopoly money left over, too.

So it's a high-spirited concert at the San Cinema this evening, once again sold out. Afterwards, David Evans, the senior British Council representative, invites us out, giving us a choice between belly dancers and moderate food, or excellent food but no belly dancing. Without debate we vote for the latter, so it's off to the banks of the Bosphorus again, this time to a restaurant in a narrow street away from the water. Again, the food is excellent. I keep off the fish, suspecting that two doses of pollution might be tempting fate.

Towards the end of the meal, when raki and wine have flowed freely, surrealism takes over. Across the room, three young Turkish couples at one table are becoming increasingly noisy. Suddenly, one of the young men throws back his head and begins a sustained howling on one undulating note. Food poisoning? Epilepsy? Metamorphosis into a werewolf? A glance at the ecstatic expression of a girl sitting opposite him discloses that he is singing her a love song. The performance draws applause not only from those round his table but others sitting nearby. Supercilious glances are cast in the direction of the phlegmatic and staid Britons across the room. National honour has been challenged. Happily we are equipped to respond. After thirteen or so years in the band of Alex Welsh, Roy Williams and John Barnes have accumulated a strong repertoire of party pieces, one of which is a duet, à la Bob and Alf Pearson, called 'Barefoot Days'. They believe the song's origins to be in Mancunian pub singalongs, but counterclaims have been made that it is sung in the South, too. Certainly the North Country elongation of syllables such as 'nook' and 'hook' give it a special flavour.

VERSE:
Do you remember . . . what times they used to be
When Dad and Mother, they'd buy new shoes for me?
All dolled up so spick and span,
Off to work we'd go hand in hand,
But the happiest days of all
Were when we wore no shoes at all . . .

CHORUS:
In barefoot days, when you and I were kids,

41

In barefoot days, oh boy, the things we did!
We'd go down to a shady nook
With a bent pin for a hook,
And we'd fish all day, fish all night,
But the bloody old fish refused to bite,
We'd slide a slide down some old cellar door,
And slide a slide till our pants got torn . . .
Then we'd have to go home and lie on our bed
While mother got busy with a needle and thread–
Oh boy, what joy we had in barefoot days!

The burst of song from an unexpected quarter silences the opposition. Indeed, when John Barnes, flushed with success, stands on a chair and intones an entire Stanley Holloway monologue (another of his specialities), the Turkish party beats a retreat, sportingly shaking our hands as they file past to the exit.

Sunday, 18 November 1979, Istanbul
Our flight to Damascus is at 10.20 a.m., but we have to leave the hotel soon after eight as the process of checking every single instrument with every single passport is a laborious one. If it doesn't already, the discipline of Yoga should include techniques for remaining calm and unruffled at airports. As a trumpet-player, I have the advantage that, as soon as I arrive in one of those vast over-heated hangars with accommodation for five thousand and seating for fifty, I can tuck the upright trumpet case under me and sit, with the brain in neutral, until everything has been sorted out.

We fly to Damascus by the Bulgarian Balkan Airline. Bruce Turner, the most unlikely-looking Stalinist at large, comes in for some ribbing on the supposition that he will get VIP treatment. To say that the in-flight meal is austere is to state an unembroidered fact. We carnivores are served a great pallid lump of compressed chicken breast garnished with a gherkin, followed by a small slab of cheese. We are agog to see how the vegetarian communist fares. His specially-ordered tray comes up. At a distance, the main course appears to be a huge, double-decker sausage roll, which cannot be. On close inspection, it turns out to be just that, but with hollow cavities where the sausages have been removed. When the steward comes round with a big tin tea-pot, like something you win at a fun-fair throwing darts at playing cards, hysteria erupts. He pours over our tea-bags water so lukewarm that it takes some prodding with the plastic spoon to elicit a small, bright orange stain—orange, because Balkan teabags incorporate grated lemon rind. In the end, the airline has its revenge on the gigglers. We approach Damascus in a series of kamikaze swoops over the desert that scare the pants off all of us.

Damascus is our first experience of a desert city. No sprawling suburbs here between airport and city centre. One minute it's a flat tarmac strip through the desert, the next a ring-road hugging the city walls on which an all-comers stock car race appears to be taking place. The chaotic scene represents a complete history of road transport through the ages. Queueing and jostling in the mid-day rush-hour are vast juggernauts, ramshackle and highly decorated coaches, gleaming Cadillacs, lorries held together by wire, battered private cars, flamboyant motor-cycles, precarious push-bikes and Biblical wooden carts drawn by donkeys. The donkeys are the only things that aren't hissing, steaming and hooting. From time to time, a car or even a full-sized truck will become frustrated at the slow progress and lumber over the central reservation to U-turn into the opposite lane. In front of us, a tiny Honda van is loaded with what seems to be the entire contents of a three-bedroomed house. Sofas and chairs and beds overlap the wheelbase by yards, but somehow it defies gravity and stays upright.

We're all fairly jugged when we reach the Omayyad Hotel. Richard Hitchcock, the British Council representative, has met us at the airport and now takes me into a corner to transact business. Am able to tell the rest that, in the Expenses Game, we are on to a winning streak in Syria. By putting us into a medium-priced Arab hotel instead of one of the big internationals, Richard has seen to it that our daily allowance, more generous than in Turkey, will leave plenty for shopping. What gives the exercise all the elements of a game at this stage is that, both in Turkey and Syria, it is illegal to take local currency out of the country. The unreality of it all is typified by the scene at Istanbul airport this morning, when I discovered that Bruce Turner had quite a bit of Turkish money left. Bruce, who calls himself the Jack Benny of jazz and has been known to drive for miles peering through a rain-drenched windscreen rather than expend electricity on the wipers, was horrified when I told him to get rid of all the loose cash before we went through customs. 'How, how?' he asked. 'Spend it,' I said. 'Go to one of the souvenir shops and buy something—anything, so long as you get rid of it.' 'But, but . . .' he mumbled in a customary expression of reluctance, 'I can't stand all that haggling.'

To add to the euphoria, there's a small snack bar attached to the hotel where we find that chunky soup and shashlik costs very little (almost everything I've eaten in the past forty-eight hours has been threaded on a stick). After eating we go to the hall—more a small lecture room than a theatre, seating about three hundred, which means that we can do the show without amplification. No need for a sound check, so we return to the hotel for a rest.

I lie on the bed and read all about Damascus from a brochure which the Omayyad Hotel provides. Splendid stuff! 'Damascus is the oldest living city in the world. Apart from this fact, it is keeping abreast with modern civilization and flurrying an accelerating tourist renaissance . . . Your visit to Damascus will unfold to you its architectural revival in its most prominent forms and fashionable adaptations . . . It still stenches with the aroma of the past . . . Visitors are flabbergasted by the splendour of the Omayyad Mosque, looking aghast at its three imposing minarets and glared by its engineering feats, decoration bravura and mosaic kaleidoscope.'

Our hopes of being flabbergasted tomorrow are set back when Richard Hitchcock arrives to collect us for the concert looking shaken. His car has just been rammed at some traffic lights by a carload of young Syrians. The driver turned out to be the sixteen-year-old son of a high-ranking military officer, who was driving without a licence. This means that instead of showing us round tomorrow, Richard has to enter into delicate negotiations to secure the cost of the damage in return for keeping the episode out of the papers. But he thinks he can get a volunteer to take his place.

The audience tonight looks from the stage to be a cosmopolitan lot. Syria is less jazz-orientated than Turkey, so my announcements have to be rather more informative than at a normal concert. But all goes well, and we get an enthusiastic reception.

Back at the hotel, it's tea in the snack bar, then bed.

Monday, 19 November 1979, Damascus
In terms of early morning decibels, Damascus is to Istanbul what a full orchestra is to a string quartet. You never heard such a din, persisting all night and rising to a Rossini-esque crescendo at dawn. There's an old *Punch* cartoon in which someone asks an Aberdonian what he does with his used razor-blades. 'Shave with 'em,' is the immediate response. Asked a similar question about his clapped-out car, the Damascan's answer would be that he drives it. Indeed, with public transport there is a system whereby state-run coaches are eventually pensioned off to private buyers, who then charge about the streets running a sort of maverick free-enterprise service. Personalized decoration is the order of the day everywhere, but nowhere more so than with these old boneshakers. A bus may not have a bonnet or bumper, but it will be embellished inside and out with painted patterns and pictures in garish fairground baroque, fairy lights, heraldic clusters of klaxons, photographs and shaggy lining material in acid colours.

Bob Straker-Cook, an education officer with the British Council, arrives in the morning to take us sightseeing. A nerve-racking task for him since, having stared appropriately aghast at the splendours of the Azem Palace and the Omayyad Mosque, we dive into the narrow and teeming passageways of the 'souk'. It's not just that the streets are crowded with people and, indeed, small cars that squeeze their way, hooting arrogantly, between the stalls. We have uncommitted wealth in our pockets, so we keep diving off into byways or lingering over the displays of gold or silk. Among the most ubiquitous and attractive craft-objects are the boxes and wooden plates covered with mosaic patterns in what looks like marquetry. I buy one in a little off-street workshop where I see that marquetry is probably the wrong word. The triangular and diamond-shaped pieces are not inlaid individually to make up the circular patterns and motifs. Strips of shaped woods and bone (or nowadays more likely plastic) are arranged in a tight bunch or 'fascis' to form the pattern, which then goes through the whole bundle like the lettering on a stick of rock. When the sticks are glued together, the resulting cylinder can be sliced like salami to produce as many wafer-thin circles of pattern as are required, and these are glued on to the wood. Garnished with mother-of-pearl, the end product can be stunning. Boxes and plates in all sizes are stacked in every tourist shop, and you have to choose carefully to find a specimen with a smooth polished surface and a lid that shuts properly. It is the decorating rather than the box-making that absorbs all the craftsmanship. Inside, hinges and screws are pretty crude.

It's going to take a little while to get to grips with Arabia. In the entrance to the Omayyad Mosque, a tall Arab with a ferocious moustache, and wearing a para-military sort of uniform, orders us peremptorily to remove our shoes. Elsewhere, women visitors are thrown a black shroud with which to cover themselves from head to foot. Ah, we think, here's that daunting severity of Islam of which we've heard. Better be careful to do it right. We shuffle round the massive hollow temple like schoolboys under threat of a whacking, boggling at the decoration bravura and mosaic kaleidoscope. Outside again and hoping to be able to find our shoes, we discover that the janitor has changed character. He now adopts a wheedling tone and tries to sell us 'worry beads' and postcards as if his next meal depends on it.

Back to the hotel for lunch, brains reeling under the sudden blitzkrieg of impressions. Refreshed by stuffed aubergine, we go out again in the afternoon to a recommended state-controlled market down the road from the hotel. No crowds and hubbub here but a quiet arcade of shops tucked away in a sunken park area. The advantage here is that prices are legally fixed, so in buying gold, jewellery and so on, there's no need to haggle. We have a field day with the Monopoly money, though everyone says that for gold we should wait until we get to the Gulf. In one shop there are large pieces of furniture—tables, chests and even a piano—covered all over in the by now

familiar mosaic veneer. A backgammon board is all I can carry. Some of us have discovered that, in the Expenses Game, maximum forfeit can be incurred if the player lands on the square marked MAKE PHONE CALL HOME. One player discovered too late that he had gone down to the tune of £40 on what amounted to no more than ritual hellos to the wife and kids.

Another enjoyable concert in the Little Theatre. Richard Hitchcock estimates that about fifty per cent of our audiences have been Syrian, the rest part of the international community. After the concert, we are invited to a party given by Bob Straker-Smith and his wife Dawn. Two taxis are ordered to take us there—someone who knows the way travels in the first one, the rest of us are supposed to follow. All the eccentricities of Damascan public transport are concentrated in our cab. The inside is an enveloping womb of thick fur, of a sickly lavender hue. Along the facia are stuck silver-framed photographs of the driver's family, and baubles hang from every knob. Right in front of the driver, the windscreen looks as if it has been struck at some time by an anti-tank missile. A huge star of cracks and splinters radiates outwards from a hole the size of a ten-pence piece. Undeterred, the driver lets in the clutch to set off in pursuit of the leading car. His cab utters a deep-throated metallic growl, arches its back for several immobile seconds and then leaps forward with an angry shriek, stalling instantly. It is clearly in deep trouble. We offer to get out and take another taxi. 'No, no, no, no, no!' cries our driver. 'Is OK!' It's quite obviously not OK—a turn of the ignition key produces another mighty leap, with a desperate gnashing of cogs deep in the engine. Perseverance brings an improvement. Instead of dying after each convulsion, the engine survives and we begin a painful, lurching pursuit in the direction in which the leading taxi disappeared long since.

It seems as if all is lost, since the driver regards our efforts to escape as a mortal affront to his professional competence. Then the other car mercifully returns to see what's happened. Still remonstrating that everything is OK, our driver is paid off and we transfer to a healthier vehicle. Relief is tinged with remorse at leaving our man stranded. 'Don't worry,' someone says, 'he'll work on it all night and be back in business in the morning.'

The party establishes a pattern with which, I suspect, we shall be all too familiar before the tour ends. 'Where have you come from? Where are you going next? How on earth do you manage to transport all the instruments? The last time I saw you was at 100 Oxford Street in, let me see . . .' The cocktail party was conceived as the perfect way to bring together a large number of people who have nothing whatever to say to each other and couldn't possibly hear it if they had. In our drummer Alan Jackson's phrase, 'It's G.B.H. of the eardrums, innit!' The cul-de-sac style of conversation reminds me of my father's complaint against an elderly friend of his, that she would insist on hailing him across a busy street with 'You must come over and meet Mr So-and-So—he's going to Asia Minor tomorrow for five years.' I am not a party man but, once there, can be relied upon to see it through to the bitter end, holding forth ceaselessly. In other words, all the foregoing is humbug. I get on famously with a lady who shares my interest in calligraphy, stuff myself to bursting point from the delicious Indian-style buffet, and corrugate every ear in the room before being dragged away to catch the transport back to the hotel.

Tuesday, 20 November 1979, Damascus
We don't have to leave until 4 p.m. and are well furnished with spare cash, so return to the souk area for shopping. Richard Hitchcock has recommended a general store opposite the Omayyad Mosque whose owner is known to him (and trusted by him). It's a tall building of several floors all looking over into a central well. In the middle of the ground floor a fountain plays, coming, the owner tells us, from a natural spring beneath the building. He offers us tea before we start our shopping and we drink it black and sweet from handle-less cups. His trading honesty reveals itself when somebody asks if the white pieces on the mosaic boxes are genuine ivory. 'Ivory, bone, plastic, who can tell these days? But if you don't know, you don't care?' Every floor is crammed with merchandise, with most of the clothing, even the Arab gear, being made in either China or India. I take a photo of Alan Jackson trying

on Arab head-dress. With his thick black eyebrows, droopy moustache and prow of a nose, he looks strikingly authentic. Silk, mosaic boxes and Egyptian kaftans, resplendent with gold braid facings, seem the best buy here.

Afterwards, a roam through the covered souk produces a classic bargaining exchange between A.J. and a shop-keeper called Victor, a stocky Damascan who claims to have visited England many times but who seems to have learnt most of his English from British soldiers from every region. His opening gambit is, 'Nice to see you, to see you, nice . . . 'Ow you doin', all right?' The subsequent conversation is peppered with English colloquialisms, the perfect foil for A.J.'s cockney jargon. The object of the haggling is a large pot or jug of indeterminate metal for which Victor wants a hundred pounds. ' 'Ow abaht it, mush?' A.J. offers fifty pounds. 'Do us a fyvour . . . One hundred pounds!' 'I can't, my son, that's all the money I've got.' 'This is much better than money—is GORGEOUS!' To Victor's suggestion that when he gets to Kuwait, A.J. can get the money without problem from his company or business associates, Alan says, 'But we're not rich men.' 'You don't 'ave to be rich!' explodes Victor, then, waxing philosophical: 'You know, the English, they used to be rich . . . I used to make a fortune out of English . . . Before— you weren't born, I think—they used to spend money without thinking . . . like this, up, down, left, right . . . but now, they can't . . . they have to be careful.' But he's soon back on his sales pitch, holding the pot up on one hand. 'You can see the harmony of the shape . . . this is good for a gentleman like you, a musician, who knows abaht it . . . you have to put in your house, is very noice . . . you can sell it for two hundred English quid in England . . . what you say?'

Alan now lowers his offer to forty pounds, which offends Victor's sense of fair dealing. 'You said just a while fifty pounds an' I don't accept it . . . now you must say over fifty!' A.J. is adamant, Victor appeals to us. 'I don't know what kind of a chance I've got with your friend—he is absolutely squeezing my neck. I have no bloody chance at all!' Eventually, Alan withdraws from the fray with, 'We'll 'ave to call it a day, my friend,' and Victor reciprocates: 'You are very welcome in Damascus . . . you are very nice people and we hope to see you many days in Damascus and I wish you nice journey.'

We troop out and set off through the crowds. Suddenly there's a shout of 'Oi!' from the distance. It's Victor, yelling 'Fifty pounds!' from his shop doorway. Without stopping, A.J. bellows 'Forty!' over his shoulder. Over a widening distance the exchange goes on. 'Fifty!' 'Forty!' 'Fifty!' There's the sound of pattering feet, and Victor runs up. 'It's OK— forty.' They go back to the shop to clinch the deal. Victor is subdued but satisfied. 'Me, I see the eggs now and not the chicken tomorrow.' It's a scrambled metaphor but we know what he means. 'As we say in England—small profit, quick return.' After some more amicable chat and a promise from A.J. to send Victor two Tootal ties for Christmas, farewells are exchanged. Walking through the souk, A.J. peers into the bag. 'Actually, I really dig this thing,' he says, with about forty pounds' worth of conviction.

I shall be sorry to leave Damascus. My sense of history is weak, but here the 'aroma of the past' is strong and irresistible. When our guide the other day casually pointed out the Street Called Straight, where Paul preached, and the East Wall over which he was lowered in a basket to escape persecution, my mind was assailed, if not by the blinding light of conversion, then at least by the strong recollection of soggy ginger biscuit dunked in milk and the shiny black books smelling faintly of petrol from which we learnt our Scriptures before breakfast at Sunningdale School. Incidentally, on one of our unaccompanied expeditions, we idiotically asked an Arab passer-by how to get to the Street Called Straight. Clearly the man had learnt his Scriptures out of a different book, and he looked totally blank. 'Straight Street?' A.J. added helpfully.

When it comes to checking out of the Omayyad Hotel, a ticklish situation develops. As the day has progressed, our passage to and from our hotel rooms has been dogged by members of the hotel staff, who indicate by wary and suspicious looks that they think we are about to do a daylight flit. The problem is that we have dissipated most of our temporary wealth and, furthermore, tipping comes under the heading of 'internal travel', which is the responsibility of the British Council. Richard Hitchcock will deal with it eventually, but he is not here yet. I try to sidestep the problem by carrying my own heavy bags to the lift. But as soon as I step outside the room a swarthy chambermaid darts from the shadows and tries to wrest them from me. Shouting at each other in two different languages, we do a sort of *paso doble* down the corridor and, at the lift, I try to extricate myself from an increasingly ugly situation by pressing what's left of my Syrian money into her hand. In the gloom of the corridor it's hard to be sure, but I have an idea that she spits. By now a male colleague has joined her, and when the lift arrives, they both get in with me, the lady now screeching with indignation over this furtive foreigner who has tried to leave without paying his dues. Down in the foyer the entire complement of chambermaids, porters, cleaners and bottle-washers has assembled, standing grimly round our luggage like guards surrounding the hostages of war. When we try to escape from embarrassment by going into the restaurant and ordering tea from our pooled resources, they post a look-out at the door in case we climb out of the window. Richard Hitchcock arrives at the very last minute and sends in his assistant Ehmad—the Arab 'fixer' with which every British Council outpost in this part of the world must be equipped if it is to function at all—to buy off the guards and release our luggage.

After farewells at the airport, we join a scrum at the boarding gates to get on the Boeing 707 to Kuwait. Men one side, women the other, use your elbows! After the comparatively libertarian ambience of Istanbul and Damascus, we are now entering the—for us—uncharted and unpredictable waters of Islam. Before leaving, we have enquired of Richard and Ehmad whether duty-free bottles of Scotch will be allowed into Kuwait—or, indeed, if their discovery will mean the dungeons and a diplomatic scandal. They reassure us. At best, the liquor will be let through, at worst it will be taken from us with nothing more than a look of withering superiority, and poured down a sink. It all depends on the prevailing winds, those affecting Kuwait at the moment being the hot breath of the Saudi Arabian Big Brother on the one side and the chill, fundamentalist breezes from Khomeini's Iran on the other.

As it happens, the problem evaporates as soon as we land. Even before we reach customs, we are met by a large, jovial Englishman called Ken Rasdall, whose speciality is supervising the opening of new airports all over the world. Kuwait has just built a whopper—a resplendent building so lofty and airy that an aircraft could happily cruise around inside it. Whilst uttering prudent and diplomatic reservations about his ability to work wonders, Ken does just that, wafting us past customs and jostling queues of immigrants to where a deputation from the British Council is waiting to greet us. An assistant representative, a Dubliner called Leo O'Keeffe hands us each a bulky sheaf of pages which turn out to contain our programme of events for the next six days. No time to read it, as we pile into a minibus to drive to the Marriott Marina Hotel.

Nothing in the itinerary nor in Leo's conversation prepares us for the pure Hollywood sight that greets us when we drive round Kuwait and reach the shores of the Persian Gulf. The Marriott Marina is a former ocean liner, now immobilized in concrete at the quayside and floodlit from end to end. At 11.30 p.m. on a warm, clear night, travel-weary spirits soar at the sight. They hit another uplifting thermal a few minutes later, when we are given in a lump sum our expenses for the six days, and a more detailed look at the itinerary shows that it is peppered with heavy point-scoring receptions and lunch invitations. One entry is mystifying—'Friday November 23: day off. Lunch with Miss Juanita Monteiro, followed by hockey match.' Glamorous expectations aroused and then nipped in the bud, all in the same sentence.

It seemed a week since A.J.'s encounter with Victor this morning, and I'm ready for sleep.

Wednesday, 21 November 1979, Kuwait

Woken at 9 a.m. by the telephone. It is Miss Juanita Monteira, who introduces herself and tells me that she used to work with my old friend Sid Dirks in what was Trans-Canadian Airlines. She will call round later to meet us in person. After a leisurely breakfast brought to the cabin by a steward, I meet the others in the foyer or fo'c's'le or whatever, for a briefing from the chief British Council representative. Dr John Munby is a live wire—in early middle-age, I suppose, but youthful, slim and slightly oriental-looking. He is keen that we should play a full diplomatic as well as musical role during our stay, and reels off a formidable list of important people whom we will meet while we're here. When he comes to Miss Juanita Monteiro, he says that she is a complete stranger to him but (looking at me), 'I understand that you know her well.' When I say in effect that I've never seen or heard of her before in my life, he looks surprised. It seems that she only attained a special mention in our itinerary because of the detailed plans she had for our welfare, from which he assumed that we were old friends. Whatever the circumstances, points are points and we accept the idea of a free lunch while expressing reservations about the hockey match. John Munby is an impressive talker, and the rush of words, often uttered while he circles one as if preparing to cut off all avenues of escape, express an energy and enthusiasm that are highly infectious. Kuwait is going to be fun.

It's a pleasant, sunny day with the temperature in the

seventies, so we go to the upper deck at noon for a swim in the small pool. The water's cool, but we have the place to ourselves as the long-term residents think it's freezing. Sunbathing afterwards, I spot a figure beckoning to me from the shadows near the entrance. It is an Indian lady of matronly build in snazzy dark glasses, floral shirt and tightly upholstered white slacks. I go over to see what she wants. 'Remember me? I called you earlier.' It is Miss Juanita Monteiro, come to meet us in person. We sit and talk about Sid Dirks, of whom it transpires that I have the more up-to-date news.

She has been in Kuwait for seventeen years, having come across from Goa (hence the Portuguese name) and, with her brother, become a member of the prosperous Indian business community. She doesn't boast to this effect, but I deduce it. In fact, she appears less flamboyant and self-assertive than her build-up in the itinerary has suggested, and she clearly wants to be as helpful as possible. We arrange to spend the day with her and her family on our rest day on Friday, and I think I have planted a fruitful seed of dissent about the hockey match.

We have a lunch date at the home of Leo O'Keeffe, and a minibus arrives at 1.30 to pick us up. Both bus and driver are at our disposal for transportation and sightseeing during our stay. The driver, whose name is John, is another Goan Indian, but of a lowlier station than the Monteiros, obviously. He's thin as a rake, with a huge black moustache the most substantial feature of his gaunt face. In his flimsy white shirt and bunched trousers, he has the fragile apprehensive look of one of Nature's victims. As we embark on the bus, he stands so rigidly to attention that he almost falls over backwards. Fresh from egalitarian England, we shake his hand and address him with jovial matiness, which clearly scares the stringy pants off him.

At first sight, Kuwait prompts the comment: 'It'll be very nice when it's finished.' Looking inland from the coast road one can see the skyscrapers and minarets and palaces of what must once have been a compact desert city. But its outlines have been blurred by overspill, and driving around on the great strips of dual-carriageway on the outskirts, there's no sense of being drawn towards a city centre. They tell us that one impressive highway shoots out into the desert and stops

56

abruptly, leading nowhere. It is on one of these busy main roads that we are bowling along in our minibus when a car suddenly cuts across our bows without warning. There's a screech of brakes and a tinkle of broken glass. A Kuwaiti army sergeant gets out, struts across with an air of exaggerated indignation and begins to upbraid John, who seems to us to make a poor show of asserting his blamelessness. In spite of—or because of—the chorus of support for John from the interior of the minibus, the man has his say and then folds his arms and leans pointedly against the front of our bus to prevent our escape. We gather that he is waiting for a police patrol to come by—a feeble hope, since within a few minutes of the impact, an impenetrable traffic jam has formed behind us as far as the eye can see. Nevertheless, the man stubbornly refuses to budge, and it is a hot and frustrating half-an-hour before he agrees to swap addresses and drive away.

When we arrive—very late—at the buffet lunch-party, they explain John's submissiveness in a situation for which the other party was so obviously to blame. It doesn't work like that here, we are told. In any contretemps between a Kuwaiti and a non-Kuwaiti, the latter is automatically to blame. And when the Kuwaiti is an army sergeant and the other party an Indian, there are even less grounds for discussion. It will take much diplomatic pleading to prevent John losing his licence and, thereby, his livelihood. No wonder he looks chronically petrified.

Another delicious buffet meal in nice company, but I can think of no way of ensuring that, when I leave at the end of these parties, I remember the names of the people I have pinioned in conversation. I like the American idea of identification tabs, but my expensive Executive Bifocals are so designed that, to read anything slightly below my eye-level, I have to get close and then throw my head back so as to squint through the bottom half of the specs. Reading a lapel-badge is pretty obvious, and when pinned to the bosom of an off-the-shoulder dress, it's positively lecherous.

With people whom I am likely to see more than once, I have a system devised years ago when I and my cousin Anthony (killed in the war) were working in the steelworks at Port Talbot. It's based on the fact that, before plastic and mass-production, toy soldiers were made of lead and hand-painted. A box of six infantrymen, for instance, would look identical from a distance but, close up, the hasty brushwork would produce recognizable differences and idiosyncracies. So that to say that two people belong 'to the same box of soldiers' gives a general idea of their build, stature and turn of feature without necessarily implying that they are identical. Example: Harold Wilson, Angus Wilson, TV's Michael Barratt and broadcaster Peter Clayton came into the world neatly packaged in the same narrow rectangular box; as did Mary Wilson, actress Kathleen Harrison of 'The Huggetts' and the lady who plays Kevin Banks's aunt in 'Crossroads'. The catering manager at the Marriott Marina Hotel is a pleasant, quiet American who comes out of the same box of soldiers as the British actor Jeremy Kemp. Until we absorb his real name, 'Jeremy Kemp' it will be.

It is Jeremy who has organized tonight's barbecue beside the large swimming pool outside the hotel. There's an audience of about three hundred of all nationalities, though they say that the nearest we come to 'local' support is a large and scattered contingent of Egyptians from the diplomatic and banking community. But there's quite a peppering of gleaming white Kuwaiti 'dishdashers' amongst the informal Western-style dress. Surveying the candle-lit scene, Bruce Turner is heard to say, 'Life for a chap, life for a chap—glamorous, glamorous.' Confronted with any kind of Hollywood lavishness, the film buff in him has little difficulty in suppresssing the Stalinist.

Glamorous it may be, it also gets decidedly chilly as midnight approaches. We notice that many of the male guests appear to have come straight from work, still carrying their brief-cases, which they lodge under the tables. As the night breeze begins to chill the jugs of soft drinks on the bar-table, they find it more and more necessary to duck under the tablecloths to consult their documents, emerging refreshed and heart-warmed by a quick glimpse of balance sheet or sales return.

Musically, it's a somewhat hybrid affair for us, since we have to temper the informative, British-orientated programme which the British Council has asked for with some of the boisterous Dixieland standards appropriate to a festive pool-side occasion. Thanks to the brief-cases and their stimulating contents, we go down increasingly well as the night progresses.

Thursday, 22 November 1979, Kuwait
Nothing to do today except go over to the British Embassy Club for a drink at mid-day and repeat the barbecue concert at the hotel tonight. Go up to the pool early—John Barnes is already there, and a small and energetic Japanese who, later in the morning, rigs up a camera on a tripod and insists on taking delayed-action photos of himself with each of us in turn. He is going to take home an odd collection of snaps—endless pictures of himself, erect and beaming, with a friendly arm round one total stranger after another.

This brisk account of events does little justice to the internal entertaining which is generated within a touring band. In leisure moments such as this morning round the pool, a team of disparate, often weary and sometimes disgruntled individuals becomes a street theatre of manic invention, augmented by fantasy characters. Much of the elaboration emanates from Mick Pyne, a devastating mimic and talented amateur cartoonist. Some years ago, on tour in Switzerland, I was passing the time in a hotel lounge doing caricatures of all and sundry. Dave Green rashly came out with: 'It's a funny thing, nobody's ever been able to do a caricature of me.' It took a few minutes' practice to remedy the deficiency with an arrangement of circles that suggested Dave in a moment of pop-eyed indignation. From then on, it became a habit to subject Dave to mild persecution by drawing the owl-like cipher in all sorts of unexpected places. The very first evening, when we were waiting for the night plane out of Basel, he visited the men's loo in the airport and encountered it staring up at him from below the water-line in the bog, where I'd scribbled it with a felt pen a few minutes earlier. I once adapted the centre-fold of a *Playboy* magazine into a Dave Green, using the boobs as bulbous eyes, and sent it to him. And every Christmas for years he has had a card from me with some kind of owl motif.

It was this spherical, glaring face that became the prototype for a character called Grosser Green, immortalized in Lyttelton Band folklore. Somewhere along the line, Mick spotted that Dave sets great store by the routine highlights of touring life, whether it's a tasty schnitzel and/or *grosser Bier* in a German or Swiss café, or a visit to the souk in the Middle East. Having set his heart on a plan, he announces it loudly and repeatedly in the hope of bringing everyone else in, but can be as quickly deflected from it by a dissenting voice. So a typical dialogue after checking in at a hotel might run:

> DAVE: 'Right, fellas . . . Grosser, Grosser!'
> SOMEONE: 'I'd sooner have a wash and a kip first . . .'
> DAVE: 'Yeah, I feel a bit shattered, too . . . right, bed, bed!'

It was from this that Grosser Green was born—a loud, barging, rotund figure with the pop-eyed, owlish features, rampaging around the world from one disaster to another. The Grosser saga has been fuelled by Dave's actual mishaps. He was once nicknamed 'Mister Bratwurst' by a German coach-driver because of his reluctance to venture further afield among the mysteries of German menus. Endless deliberation and vacillation at the table would always end with: 'No, I think I'll just have a Bratwurst.' It was a red-letter day when he decided to give himself a treat, plumping for something German in the fish section which, for sheer weight of consonants and syllables, promised to be substantial. The metamorphosis into Grosser, all saucer eyes and indignant cries of 'WHA-A-A-AT???', was instantaneous when the waiter arrived with two cold roll-mops on a plate. Thenceforward, in restaurants all over the world, the words 'I've done it again' have disclosed that Grosser has once more backed a loser. The whole of this is a foul calumny on Dave's sensitive, talented and long-suffering nature, but he takes it well and indeed acts up to it.

The foil for Grosser's excesses is provided by the ineffably smooth Lord de Vere, a role for which Roy William's erect stance and Wellingtonian nose suit him perfectly. Lord de Vere is related, none too distantly, to Grytpype-Thynne of the Goons, whose drawling, 'Steady, Neddy' has, in his Lordship,

been exaggerated into an aristocratic slaughter of vowels—
'Ste-ah-de-ah, Ne-ad-de-ah.'

In these fantasies Mick Pyne plays a variety of roles, all of
them hilarious and in stark contrast to the persona of
Exploding Pianist which emerges in more depressive moments.
Chris Pyne, who was with me for some time on trombone,
once said, 'I have to admit that my brother operates on a very
short fuse.' We've had a few tiffs over ten years or so, but
many more laughs—and of course, fabulous music.

The Embassy Club, to which we're taken at noon, turns out
to be a very informal affair—an out-building in the British
Embassy grounds with a rectangular bar-room that succeeds in
reproducing all the homely discomfort of the English pub—
not enough room, not enough seats and a scrum round the bar
counter. The invitation has come from two members of the
Embassy staff who, John Munby says, are of great assistance in
the British Council's work. Nuri Alvarez and G. Sarwar are
Iraqi and Pakistani respectively, but close enough in build and
outline to appear quite convincing book-ends at a distance.
Talking to Mr Sarwar about Pakistani restaurants in London,
we get on to the subject of food in the Middle East. 'Of
course,' he says, 'you are unlikely to eat any actual Arab food
during your stay here—what you get in hotels and private
houses will be derived from Lebanon to the West, Persia to the
North and India to the East. So you'll be familiar with it all
from your Cypriot and Indian restaurants.' So, no sheeps'
eyes, then.

After an extended liquid lunch with typical pub chat among
the homesick expatriates, it's back to the Marriott for more
lounging until tonight's show. This is identical to last night's,
except that Nuri is on hand, beckoning us over to his table
whenever he thinks a dip into his briefcase will do us good.

We get English language newspapers delivered with breakfast
at the Marriott, and they are not making very comfortable
reading at the moment. Since November 4, when Iranian
students invaded the US Embassy in Tehran and took a
hundred hostages, the situation has been tense throughout the
Gulf. Now we hear that, two days ago, a group of fanatics
invaded the Grand Mosque in Mecca, claiming that their
leader is the Mahdi who, according to prophesy, is come to

purify Islam. I have been making regular visits to the hotel reception desk to see if there is an urgent message from the British Council in London calling off our visit to Jeddah, but nothing has arrived. They are obviously reading different papers in London—the Gulf *Times* reports the whole affair in terms of deep crisis. One of the incentives to keep a day-to-day diary is the keen anticipation of one day having something sensational to write in it.

Friday, 23 November 1979, Kuwait

Our free day. Juanita arrives at 11 a.m. to take us out for the day, driving a handsome Buick. John has been booked for the day with the minibus so we travel in convoy to what would have been a leafy suburb of Kuwait had there been a leaf in sight. Kuwait is growing so fast that if you wake up in the dead of night you can hear it groaning in labour. With houses going up at such a rate, there is no time to tart up the surrounds. So smart villas stand in rows in the desert dust, waiting in vain for the tree-lined avenues and broad drives and pavements appropriate to their station in life. We stop at one of them and, inside, are introduced to two Indian couples with curiously English names—Joe and Evelynn, Ozzie and Hazel. Joe is Juanita's brother, who came to Kuwait from Goa twenty-seven years ago and has clearly thrived in business ever since. We have drinks round a cocktail bar festooned with comic pub notices from England, saucy slogans in framed Gothic script or poker-work.

Ozzie, an elegant figure in early middle-age with greyish-white hair, tells me that he was at the Regal Cinema, Edmonton, in 1957 on the night I sat in for a number with Lionel Hampton's Band, wearing a fashionable Edwardian-style suit that prompted one Teddy Boy punter to say 'That 'Umphrey—'e's one of us!' Ozzie had a front-row seat in the reserved VIP section. He was still wondering why they had ushered him there without even looking at his ticket when the curtain went up, and he saw the whole Lionel Hampton Band dressed in blue gaberdine suits identical to his. He had been taken for one of their entourage and favoured accordingly.

Other guests are expected for lunch, so we go down to a games room in the basement and play darts, table-tennis and billiards while we wait. They don't turn up, so, suitably exercised, we return upstairs and sit down to a sumptuous Indian banquet. I can't list the menu—all Indian dishes look alike to me—but it would have been enough just to sit and look at the vivid still-life of autumnal browns, reds, oranges and yellows. The most damning evidence of the insensitivity of the British Raj was that horrible greenish mess, unaccountably laced with sultanas and bits of hard-boiled egg, which, as a schoolboy, I was taught to call 'curry'. Musicians, forced to eat at peculiar hours, were well ahead of the *Good Food Guide* in finding the best Indian restaurants when they began to proliferate in the late Fifties. It was only then that I discovered that 'curry' was not something to be relegated, with tapioca pudding and boiled parsnips, to the limbo of Things Best Forgotten, but represented a rich variety of delicious flavours enhanced by colours that should leave the tablecloth looking like an oriental action painting. Before we tuck in, Joe invites us to make ourselves completely at home, to which Dave Green is heard to say, through a mouthful of vegetable samosa, 'I don't eat like this at home!'

Happily, the delayed lunch has put the hockey match out of the question, so we debate what we will do with the rest of the afternoon. Some are so crippled by vindaloo and dhansak that they choose to retire with John and the minibus to the hotel. John Barnes, Alan Jackson and I decide that we would like to see 'the desert', envisaging that somewhere beyond the outskirts of town there must be arid dunes and camels and Ronald Colman. From the aeroplane at night all we saw was an inky blackness punctuated dramatically by flare-ups from scattered oil wells. Juanita volunteers to drive us out there, suggesting, somewhat vainly, that we might like to take in a guided tour of an oil refinery too. It takes a while to get clear, first of buildings and then of the discarded Pepsi tins, car tyres and oil cans that contribute to an aura of litter all around the city. After driving for about forty minutes we reach a point where, if you stand with your back to an unsightly oil installation on the horizon, the remaining three-quarters of the vista is uninterrupted desert. It's still rather disappointing –

very flat and with dirty-grey, scrubby sand, nothing like the Sahara. Nevertheless, it inspires J.B. to pose for photos in Beau Geste style, prostrate on the sand and clawing for water.

Further down the road we spot, over to our right, the long brown rectangle of a Bedouin tent. Responding to our interest, Juanita swings off the road and charges towards it across the sand. We park at a discreet distance and get out. Immediately a cloud of dust on the horizon heralds the appearance of a herd of lop-eared Arabian sheep at a brisk gallop, pursued by a boy who turns out to be the eldest son of the family, hurrying back to find out who these intruders are. As a woman comes out of the tent to meet us, with a small girl hiding in the folds of her voluminous robes, two younger boys with more sheep make a miraculously fast appearance from nowhere. Had the paterfamilias been there, we might have benefited from some of that spontaneous hospitality for which the Bedouin are renowned. But the likelihood is that he works in an oil installation and will return tonight, parking a Mercedes alongside the tent. As it is, our converse is limited. In an effort to bridge the language gap, I fish out my Casio musical calculator and play the little girl a tune. She looks at me with wide-eyed incredulity and then, turning away, buries her face in her mother's pelvic region. Still, we are able, at a respectful distance, to peer at the pots and pans in the huge open tent. A.J. sums it up. 'Dead ephnic, innit!' After sundry gestures of salutation, we leave them in peace.

Back at the hotel around 6 o'clock, we get ready to go to a reception at John Munby's house. A swinging affair, thanks to John and Lilian M.'s energy as hosts and a lanky and highly-strung Palestinian doctor who has brought along an armful of Louis Armstrong records. A fine cross-section of nationalities and characters, several of whom, like Fred Steele ('Jeremy Kemp') and the heavenly twins Nuri and Mr Sarwar from the British Embassy, we have met before.

Several Kuwaitis are here in their gleaming white dish-dashers. Two arrive holding hands, arousing some unworthy Western speculation. 'You'll have to learn about the Arab handholding,' says John Munby reprovingly, going on to explain that it represents a prolonged handshake indicating that the men are established friends rather than just aquaintances. I am introduced to one (with a short handshake) and spend some time chatting. He shares with an erstwhile Turkish waiter at Chaglayan's Kebab House in Hendon the disconcerting habit of punctuating his conversation with 'Sorry, sorry,' as if apologising in advance for his sentiments. 'Sorry . . . sorry . . . you must understand that I am a Shi'ite Muslim, but . . . sorry . . . I do not . . . sorry, sorry . . . approve of Khomeini . . .' It occurs to me while he's talking that there must be available some rather inexact Asian equivalent of Roget's *Thesaurus* that equates 'sorry' with 'excuse me', and that both my Kuwaiti acquaintance and the Hendon waiter are simply asking for allowances to be made for their poor English. In the light of the purges going on in Iran, 'I do not approve of Khomeini' seems a mild way of putting it. It transpires not unexpectedly that money is at the root of his disapproval. He owns a rich fabrics empire that stretches to India, Thailand and Japan, and needs all the favourable PR he can get. I discover while we're talking why Arab eyes flash so prodigiously. It's not simply the blackness of the eyebrows, though they and the ubiquitous black moustache do bestow a certain ferocity on the mildest of faces. It's the whites of the eyes that impress—no hint of the burst grape look that Western eyes acquire from a conspiracy of nicotine and hangover, but absolutely clear and with a hint of robin's egg blue.

A dominant figure at the party is another berobed Arab, an outsize version of Dizzy Gillespie with the same swivel-eyed look that contrives to blend mockery with innocence. When I first encounter him, he is in earnest conversation with a man from the BBC to whom I am introduced. I linger on to eavesdrop. Dizzy is explaining that, 'though it is not in our culture to show off', his family should rightfully be ruling Kuwait. He goes on to say that his uncle was the first Arab to get a degree at Oxford-and-Cambridge—I've hyphenated them because he speaks as if they were one single institution. While he talks, the BBC man studies his face intently, presumably trying to divine whether he is hearing the truth or an outrageous 'line'. Dizzy's swivelling eyes give nothing away.

Later, I ask John Munby who he is. 'We're not absolutely sure,' he says. 'He turns up at all the parties, and I think he works for the Ministry of Education. We suspect he might be deputed to keep a benevolent but watchful eye on us.' Dizzy certainly likes to give that impression. When he is later introduced to us all, the eyes roll across to give us a knowing sideways look. 'I have seen most of you before,' he says. 'You left the hotel yesterday at eleven o'clock, a lady was with you.' The Marriott Hotel stands aloof from other buildings. To have seen us leave with Juanita, he must either have been lurking behind potted palms in the foyer or perched high on a distant skyscraper with binoculars. We begin to watch our words. There are only a handful of people left when he finally takes his leave. I tell him that I am giving an illustrated talk tomorrow in which I shall solicit questions from the audience. Round come the eyes again. 'I shall be there. Expect a question.' Despite his cultivated air of genial menace, the room seems to be empty after he has finally swept out. But not for long—two minutes later he sweeps back and settles down to hold forth into the night. If indeed he is a watchdog for the Government, he certainly enjoys his job.

Saturday, 24 November 1979, Kuwait
Early breakfast, then up to the upper deck pool to swim. It's a rather muggy morning and the flies are out in force. Fortunately, there is another Marina Hotel pool 'ashore' where we played for the barbecue, and this is less infested so we transfer en masse, feeling Dizzy's binoculars boring into the back of our necks as we walk across. In mid-morning, Juanita turns up, bringing me a large floppy textbook on colloquial Arabic which the Kuwait Oil Company issues to its foreign employees. I had mentioned yesterday that I wanted to learn some words in Arabic with which to ingratiate myself with audiences over here, and this is her generous response. After she's left, I study the first few pages, and end up with a string of words which, the book assures me, represent an appropriate greeting. There is a phonetic guide, so I am soon able to rattle off 'Marhaba . . . masa' al-kher . . . ahlan wa sahlan'. I rather wish they didn't translate as 'Hello, good evening and welcome,' but perhaps I can switch them round a bit.
At lunch over a club sandwich I try 'Shukran' ('Thank you')

out on the waiter. He responds with what sounds like "Ave one', a dangerous invitation to travelling Brits. A riffle through the book reveals that he is saying 'Afwan', rather improbably translated as 'Not at all'. At least they don't say 'You're welcome'! The waiter shows interest in my book, sits down to study it with me. He is Egyptian, so queries some of the Kuwaiti phonetic pronunciation, but I have a useful lesson in some of the infinite variety of guttural sounds that the language demands. They vary from a gentle rasp to what, on the streets of London, would be taken as the prelude to a spit, and the meaning of words depends on their exactness. By the time he's called away to another table I've got 'Hello, good evening and welcome' off pat.

Driver John is supposed to pick us up at 5 p.m. but he doesn't appear. We have to go to the Mousetrap Theatre in the English School to set up for tonight's lecture, so Nuri is contacted at the British Embassy. He sends an Embassy estate wagon to collect the instruments, and we hire two cabs to follow it.

The Mousetrap Theatre is inside a compound, approached across a wide expanse of dusty open space. A tiny staircase leads down to the backstage area. The cars have to park outside the compound, so all the gear has to be taken over by hand. A gnarled and wiry Arab caretaker is sent across to help. The drums are no problem, but Dave Green's electric 'pogo stick' bass is transported in a narrow rectangular box over six feet long and weighing a ton. Having reconnoitred the tiny entrance, I collect a few helpers to go and fetch it. Approaching us across the quadrangle is a strange apparition, half man, half sideboard. It's the caretaker, bent in a right angle at the waist, with Dave's case on his back. All we can see of him is a pair of matchstick legs, bowing slightly under the weight. Brushing aside our offers of help, he teeters on single-handed, leaving us to speculate as to how he got the thing on his back in the first place.

The lecture-concert is an idea of John Munby's, presumably to underline the educational and cultural aspect of British Council tours and to offset the two purely commercial barbecues with which our Kuwait stint began. Everyone here is full of admiration for John's energy, and for the way in which he has worked to make the Council activities self-sufficient instead of just wringing his hands over the parsimony of the Foreign Office. As a result we have the feeling that we are doing something worthwhile and constructive. I must say I'm enjoying the public relations bit, and I've been looking forward to tonight's performance. Apart from an opening gambit I have nothing prepared—my usual technique in 'talks' is to rely on questions, and if nobody asks any, to pose them myself and to go on to answer them . . . eg: 'I can see you're wondering how we know when to stop and start' or 'You may well ask how much of our performance is improvised and how much prepared.'

In the event, there are quite a few spontaneous questions along those lines—though the loaded and possibly incriminating question that Dizzy seemed to be threatening last night doesn't materialize, as he fails to show up. With the adrenalin flowing, I talk relentlessly, and nobody seems to mind. Afterwards it is into cars and off to a buffet party at Ken Rasdall's house. Ken and his wife Anne represent one of the great bonuses of the touring life—instant friends, one might call them, who from the first meeting are ready with help, hospitality and company, yet remain sensitive to one's occasional need for solitude, silence and rest. Every musician and every band has an honourable roster of Ken and Annes, Len and Pats, Dennis and Celias, Tom and Helens, Doug and Adeles—I quote at random from our own list over the years— with whom this special relationship is forged virtually on sight in backstage or theatre bar meetings, and held together by a tenuous chain of Christmas cards and overseas postcards. It's a rich reward for doing no more than one's job.

We have a memorable curry and much more besides at the Rasdalls' and stay long enough in congenial company to work it off before retiring.

Sunday, 25 November 1979, Kuwait
Driver John reappears this morning, looking subdued and tearstained after a severe reprimand and threat of the sack from Nuri. It transpires that he went to a family party yesterday lunchtime, got smashed and was sleeping it off when

69

he should have been taking us to the theatre. A peccadillo by British standards, and we are surprised by the severity of the retribution and by John's reaction to it.

We leave the hotel at 11 a.m. to go with the instruments to the Telecomunications Centre, where tonight's last concert is to be held. There an Arab caretaker makes us lemon tea while we set up and organize the sound and lighting. We have to get it all done early because there is a lunch with John Cambridge, the British Ambassador, at the Embassy. We fear a rather stuffy, formal affair, since bigwigs from the local banking and diplomatic community are going to be there. It turns out to be the opposite—a queue-up and help-yourself buffet (curry again—my taste buds are now permanently steaming)—with John Cambridge, a lively and unstuffy bachelor, greeting everyone with 'Jackets off—it's far too hot to wear jackets!' There is a lot of talk about the tense situation in Saudi Arabia to which we listen with ears flapping since we are due to fly in there in three days' time. Views are divided—the diplomats are sanguine in the belief that it will all blow over, the bankers and businessmen—with cash involved—have long faces. No one seems to think we have a hope in hell of being let in, and I must say that the idea of a British jazz band breezing into a situation that the local Press is describing variously as 'a land-mine', 'a tinder box' and 'a knife's edge' does seem rather far-fetched. But in Arabia nothing is predictable, and from our British Council mentors in London not a word has been heard.

We get back to the hotel at 3 p.m. One or two of us, feeling that by now the alimentary canal is clogged from terminal to terminal with curry, decide to visit an exhibition of Bedouin Art at the Kuwait National Museum, which is visible along the coast road from the hotel. In the process we discover something else about Arabia. The combination of flat, featureless scenery, extended horizons and desert haze plays havoc with one's sense of distance. What looked like a pleasant, twenty-minute amble ended up as an hour's hard slog over what must have been three miles of dusty road—and at the end of it, the Museum was closed for the afternoon. We took a taxi back.

Backstage at the Telecommunications Centre this evening an old acquaintance turns up—Carl Robert, who used to work at Granada TV when we did our 'Here's Humph' series in

Manchester, and who now works with Kuwait Television. In conversation, we ask him which is the best place for buying dishdashers (not only for souvenir value but because they look so comfortable). He takes rough measurements and colour preferences, dashes off and returns to present us with one each before the concert starts.

The concert is a sell-out, about five hundred people. My 'Marhaba . . . masa' al-kher . . . ahlan wa sahlan' earns appreciative applause from the Arab-speaking members of the audience and not too much laughter from the rest.

Party at home of Marc Coulon—more splendid curry, nice people.

Monday 26 November 1979, Kuwait
We don't have to leave for Dubai until around 4 o'clock this afternoon, so there is time for a shopping expedition. Thanks to the hospitality we've received here we have amassed a handy number of expenses points. Bruce Turner has, needless to say, ascertained that in this temporal context you *can* take it with you, there being no currency restrictions between countries in the Gulf. We go into a well-rehearsed routine. 'Aren't you coming to buy presents for the family?' 'NEVER! Sooner have a tooth pulled, tooth pulled!' 'D'you mean you're not taking anything back for the little woman?' 'Yeah . . . a peck on the forehead, peck on the forehead!' Some of our party go with Juanita to a modern souk at Salameeyah a little way out of town, the rest take John and the minibus into the centre of Kuwait to wander around there.

We have been told that the gold souk is something to see, but even so it takes us by surprise. It doesn't exist on its own, but is simply an area in one corner of the covered market in which all the tiny gold shops are concentrated. The first impression, funnily enough, is of cheap vulgarity, of windows crammed with tier upon tier of trashy bracelets and Christmas cracker rings. It arises, first, because no jeweller in his right mind at home would display so much valuable stock in a window without elaborate and visible security measures and, secondly, because none of the gold here is less than 18 carat which means that, *en masse*, it has an unconvincing orange

71

colour. Buying gold is a simple and safe exercise here—the trade is strictly supervised, the prices are calculated on weight alone, with nothing added for design or workmanship, and you pay according to the day's published international gold price. Once the truth has dawned that the cluster of Aladdin's caves are stocked with the real thing, fantasy takes over. Objects displayed with such profligacy and abandon must be dirt cheap, I'll have two dozen bracelets and a quarter of a pound of gold rings, please, don't bother to wrap them, I'll put 'em on here. The cure is to go in and make a transaction. Visions of sneaking through the Customs at Heathrow with an armful of negotiable bullion vanish when you discover how many grams a quite flimsy-looking bracelet will notch up on the scales. I succumb to gold fever and buy myself an 18-carat ring. I've never worn a ring in my life, but the opportunity to look flash for a mere £20 outlay can't be passed up. When I buy a bracelet, too, to take home, I am brought heavily down to earth as the rather supercilious Indian behind the counter asks, 'Only one?' I know what he means—in the street and at the airport we have seen Arab women wearing a dozen or so on each wrist, the flashing gold against the sombre black shrouds indicating a compact between God and Mammon.

Apart from the gold and the hi-fi shops, where cassette recorders are strikingly cheap, the rest of the souk is disappointing—acres of gaudy, sub-Woolworth junk. John Barnes stops off at a men's wear stall to equip himself, from head to foot, with Arab gear. The salesman takes great delight in dressing him up, there and then, and at the end J.B. looks quite convincing with his dark glasses and jutting beard.

Back at the hotel at lunchtime, John and Lilian Munby call in to say goodbye. As the hotel's public rooms offer rather scattered seating, we repair to my cabin for an impromptu farewell party. It's largely through John's enthusiasm that this stint in Kuwait has been so enjoyable. The cold fact is that, compared with Turkey and even Syria, there is a negligible indigenous audience for jazz in the Gulf, and yet we end this six-day stint with the distinct impression that we have met, talked with and played to a large variety of nationalities outside of the expatriate clique.

Talking to John Munby we discover the reason for driver

John's tragic reaction to his reprimand the other morning. Everything in the diplomatic and business sphere of activity here is run on such a tight rein that dereliction of duty such as failing to turn up for work means, for the lower ranks, eventual dismissal. That in turns means deportation back to India, since immigrants from the subcontinent can only stay if they have employment. Despite the pig-in-the-middle situation in which they find themselves, booted about by the Arabs and by foreigners of every nationality as well as by compatriots higher up the success ladder, they achieve and export for their families at home a far higher standard of living than they could expect in India. So dismissal is not just a set-back but a disaster. Being fresh from a Britain which is, by comparison, egalitarian we find it shockingly Dickensian and plead with John Munby on driver John's behalf, extracting a grudging and not very convincing promise that he will give him another chance. Kuwait is at present one of the more easy-going of the Arab states, but the fear which keeps John in a rigid posture of colonial subservience spreads upwards through the whole expatriate community, except among those too bullishly insensitive to see the eventual crunch coming. Arabia is for the Arabs, and everyone else is here on sufferance. 'Dizzy's' whole act at the party the other night amounted to a gleeful exercise in scaring the daylights out of influential and highly-placed Europeans who nevertheless don't quite know where they stand.

It's late evening when we go to Kuwait Airport for the flight to Dubai. Ken Rasdall is there to see us off, and Leo O'Keeffe, too, though he doesn't see much of us as Bruce Turner discovers that he's left his spectacles on the minibus and it's Leo who has to speed off in his car to try and intercept them on the way back to Kuwait. I feel slightly end-of-the-hols about leaving Kuwait—under John Munby's aegis it's been a stimulating week.

This feeling is accentuated when we get to Dubai. We have a long queue at immigration because an Iranian plane has just come in and everyone is being screened carefully. We're met by several young men from the Jebel Ali Club, where we are to play tomorrow. Jebel Ali is a 'village' about twelve miles from Dubai which has been built to house the personnel of the international construction company which is building a vast new harbour there. The Club has hired us from the British Council for this gig, and I soon gather from Dave, the Club secretary, that this will be a predominantly expatriate audience. I've begun to enjoy the quasi-diplomatic aspect of our tour, and my feeling is that there'll be little scope for it here.

When we get to Jebel Ali and walk into the Club room with all our bags, there's a full-scale disco in progress, celebrating someone's anniversary. We're invited to help ourselves from the bar and buffet, which is appreciated, but no one is in the mood for a party after a long day. 'Boys' are summoned to take our bags to the accommodation that's been arranged—they turn out to be mature and, in some cases, middle-aged Indians who are ordered about like office juniors. When I ask tentatively if there are likely to be any Arabs at tomorrow's concert, the answer is emphatic. 'Good God, no!' Clearly we are in a different atmosphere here.

But the generosity is unbounded. We're being housed here in two 'executive bungalows' at no expense, and there is an open invitation to eat all meals in the Club. What with that and the hospitality at the disco, spirits rise from the floor. I'm sharing one bungalow with John Barnes and Roy Williams, and it is John's idea that, in the middle of the night, we should dress up in the various bits of Arab gear that we've bought and pay a call on the others in their bungalow along the way. Under cover of darkness, we flit across the scrubby sand and knock imperiously on their door. Dave Green answers it, and for a second or two his eyes become twin spheres of alarm. A.J., who is already in bed, reaches for his Instamatic. 'That's great—I gotta get a picture of this!' He shoots away from a reclining position, laughing so much that he's unlikely to get more than a blur.

Tuesday, 27 November 1979, Dubai

The weather this morning is English summerish, hot but with no humidity. There's a swimming pool alongside the Club, empty like the pools in Kuwait because the residents think it's cold. We lounge around it during the morning. Bruce Turner, who would as soon buy a phial of liquid gold as a bottle of sun oil, burnt himself in patches at Kuwait, so he lies on the slatted sun-bed here with the affected parts covered by bits of his discarded clothing—T-shirt over the forehead, underpants round the neck, socks draped over the tops of the feet. He looks like a mummy that's come unwrapped.

Lunch of steak and jacket potatoes in the Club, then we are picked up for a sight-seeing trip into Dubai, with British Council man, Jim Mollison, and his assistant Jan as guides. On the way we see our first camel—moth-eaten like even the noblest of its species and with a pronounced limp, but a camel nonetheless. We take a ride up the Creek in one of the ferry motor-barges. Those that simply ply from one side to the other are packed with people perched on every flat surface, but since we hire one for a more extended sightseeing trip we have it to ourselves. The Creek, notorious for gold-smuggling operations in the not very distant past, sounds romantic but is to all appearances just a broad river flanked by huge hotels and corporation offices. The Gulf must be an architects' Paradise. With no 'architectural heritage' with which to conform and almost infinite space, ideas can run riot, and we pass some magnificently far-out buildings, all spreading wings and jutting spearheads, that seem about to take off into the sky. The water's edge is lined with clusters of boats of all shapes, from cabin cruisers to creaking wooden dhows and rusty cargo ships. With hygienic nicety the dhows have outboard loos—rickety wooden 'boxes' projecting on wooden brackets from the stern in which the incumbent crouches, suspended over the sea. A.J. is delighted to spot, in the mêlée of boats, a cabin cruiser bearing the name JACKSON.

Over in the souk there's a mixture of the exotic and the trashy similar to that which we found in Kuwait. For a true whiff of Arabia the best spot is the spice souk, where heaps of ground turmeric, saffron, cumin, cayenne pepper, nutmeg, in a spectrum of autumnal shades give off an intoxicating and sneeze-inducing aroma. In a tiny clothing shop I complete my Arab wardrobe by buying a full head-dress assembly. There's the small filigree skull-cap that goes on first—like the Jewish skull-cap, it has religious significance and is the item that's likely to give offence if worn irreverently. Over this goes the scarf head-dress, the square of white nylon or chequered woven silk that is folded into a triangle and draped over the head with the centre of the hypotenuse forming a peak. On top of this goes the double coil bound in black thread and tasselled which perches on the head and, with a simple combination of weight and blind faith, stops the whole assembly from being whisked off by the first gust of wind. If the Arab shopkeeper feels any resentment at decking out Western infidels in the national head-dress, he doesn't show it, demonstrating with great care and good humour how the pieces should be worn. I snap Dave trying on his headgear and wearing the resigned look of someone who knows that the result will fuel the Grosser legend.

The evening concert is in the tarmacked forecourt of the Club, open to the skies except for a covered bandstand. When A.J. unpacks his drums to set up, he finds one head of the snare drum split right across, possibly as a result of the heat earlier today. The Club secretary sends one of the Indian servants off in a land-rover to the only music shop in the Emirate of Dubai. Since the most modern instruments we saw at the shops were ethnic Bedouin souvenir tom-toms made of (presumably) camel-hide, we hold out little hope, but the land-rover returns with a repaired drum within an hour. There's a further short, sharp panic just before the concert when, lulled into unusual sloppiness by a burst of pre-concert hospitality at the bar, I take the trumpet out with two minutes to go and find the valves locked rigid. There are two possible explanations. It could have had a knock during the minute or two when it was taken out of my hands by a porter back at the Marriott Hotel. Or in the dry heat of the day it could simply have seized up. Hoping for the latter, I put a well-rehearsed emergency routine into action. It's a mad dash to the chalet, on with the bathroom shower and a quick drenching for the trumpet, bell upwards, which immediately releases everything, including my knotted nerves, and has me back on stage at the appointed time, ready for action.

The club forecourt is packed with an almost exclusively British expatriate audience most of whom, judging from snatches of conversation en route to the stage and during the interval, passed through the Humphrey Lyttelton Club at 100 Oxford Street during the Fifties. This is encouraging and at the same time daunting, since some Oxford Street veterans believe that the modest entrance fee to Mack's Restaurant bought them a lifetime's guarantee that my music would never change so much as a dotted quaver. Ideally, they would like to have had the whole ambience—the band, the grotty murals, the geriatric staff—preserved in jars of formalin like biological specimens, to keep the nostalgia unimpaired. Fortunately, it's rarity that's the winning card tonight, and the very fact that we suddenly materialize in their midst is enough to unleash cheering euphoria. A good thing, because the forecourt has acoustic peculiarities—the fully amplified sound dies in the night air a few yards out from the stage, which means that the music can't reach the back of the audience without deafening the front rows. Nevertheless, by the end it's all a wild success.

Wednesday, 28 November 1979, Dubai
More lounging by the pool in the morning, then into Dubai again at lunchtime for a reception with the British Consul at the Embassy. Lovely setting for buffet lunch round the pool,

hedged in by trellised greenery. Curry again, but absolutely delicious. While I eat, I give an interview to a young lady from the Embassy who also contributes to *What's On in Dubai*. Hear a good (true) story apropos the formality of Arab greetings, which extend far beyond the few sentences I learnt in Kuwait. Some months ago the international school across the road from the Embassy caught fire. The pupils and staff were hurriedly evacuated and the fire brigade sent for. When the appliances arrived the fire chief went over to the headmaster and embarked on a string of felicitations, calling down the blessings of Allah on the man himself, his wife, children, friends, animals, car and household goods. It was only when these had been exchanged with measured deliberation that the firemen then became galvanized into action with their hoses.

Speaking of urgency, we have still had no word from the British Council in London about our imminent trip to Jeddah. Most people here think that, with fundamentalist fever affecting even such easy-going places as Kuwait and Dubai, the notion of our playing in the grounds of the British Embassy in Jeddah is unlikely to say the least. However, we shall match London's stiff upper lip when we leave for Saudi Arabia tonight. The departure time from Jebel Ali is 7.30, so there is time to rest before saying our liquid farewells in the Club. It's my bad luck that I am sharing my bungalow with ex-Alex Welsh Band members who, like former colleague Lennie Hastings, are Richard Tauber freaks. John Barnes, with a coin in his eye as a monocle, has an after-lunch attack of the Taubers that aggravates even Roy Williams who is trying to sleep. But there's no stopping J.B. when he gets his teeth into 'You are my Heart's Delight'!

The exit customs at Dubai airport are the toughest yet. They search all the hand-baggage thoroughly, turning out everything on to the counter and leaving us to put it all back. Passing under the metal-detector arch I set off a burst of urgent bleeping caused, it transpires, by my wine-waiter's knife, a constant companion. I don't suppose many people fly into Saudi Arabia equipped with blade, corkscrew and lever, and it looks at one point as if they are about to confiscate it. I use it most at home for cutting calligraphy pens from garden cane, so it does have a very sharp and dangerous blade. On the other hand, Arab writing is done with a 'reed' pen exactly like my homemade product, so they should know all about pen-knives. And presumably the senior official to whom the matter is referred does, because I get the knife back. Dave Green doesn't materialize on the plane, and we fear we may have lost him. He eventually arrives in full Grosser manifestation, eyes popping with indignation. The customs man has just prised open several of his boxes of Turkish Delight which have been intact since Istanbul.

The women go on board first, and when our turn comes, we half expect to see them all segregated at the back of the plane. In fact, they are scattered around to be joined by their menfolk, and I can only assume that the separation at the gate was to avoid any unseemly jostling and bodily contact. Contrary to expectations, the atmosphere on the plane is quite skittish. Since in Saudi Arabia women are forbidden to work, we had expected the plane to be staffed by stern men, but it seems that the law doesn't stretch to foreign women thirty thousand feet above the ground, and there are air-hostesses of several nationalities. John Barnes is still in festive mood, flirting with the Indian stewardess and generally clowning around. It prompts our first whiff of Islamic austerity. A Saudi Arab next to Mick Pyne and Roy Williams turns to them and asks, 'Who is this man? Why does he wish us to laugh?' What little I know about Arab humour so far comes from a short and abortive involvement in a cartoon-film that animator Richard Williams was once preparing, based on the legendary tales of Nasruddin Hoca. Part sage, part fool, Nasruddin is the subject of anecdotes in every Islamic country from Turkey round to Tunisia, and pretty heavy and oblique stuff I found them in translation. Far removed, in fact, from the sharp attacks of the Frank Randalls to which J.B. is prone!

We have to break our journey and go through more customs at Dahran, and Dave's face as he emerges from inspection tells us that more of his Turkish Delight has been vandalized. It turns out not to be his night. On the way round he has been recording sounds and impressions of the tour on cassette. When we arrive after the second leg at Jeddah, he rather imprudently walks into the customs hall with the recorder running, hoping to capture our arrival for posterity. He must have captured some good material, too, because the men at the customs counter are quite jolly, especially when one of them finds a programme for the tour in a suitcase and sets about matching the musicians to their photos in the brochure. But as we move on, one of the men spots the little red recording light flashing away, and pounces. Without saying anything, he holds out his hand for the recorder, presses the eject button, removes the cassette and walks off with it.

A quiet young Scot called Jim McGrath welcomes us, and takes us to the Sands Hotel, which will be our home for the next four days.

Thursday, 29 November 1979, Jeddah
This stint in Jeddah is not being run by the British Council but is a private arrangement with the Jeddah Concert Committee, a voluntary body, recruited from the British, German and Australian Embassies, which puts on drama shows on an outdoor stage in the grounds of the British Embassy. This morning a tall and taciturn Australian called Ian Palmeter comes round to make contact and brief us about the concerts. There is a general air of depression around today, compounded of tiredness, a feeling of anticlimax after the lively social atmosphere in both Kuwait and Dubai, and a consciousness not hitherto felt of being in an alien and not very hospitable culture. In other words, the vibes are not good. No tangible reason—the hotel is very comfortable and the Lebanese management quite friendly and amenable.

Later in the morning we are driven half a mile along a dusty road to the Embassy where there is a scaffolded stage just inside the main gate. We are also shown the way to the swimming pool which we are invited to use whenever we like. Other members of the concert committee are there, including the British representative Tim King, who anticipates a large crowd tonight. We get lifts back to the hotel and have lunch in the all-day coffee shop, which has a flamboyantly descriptive menu. I choose an 'Open Faced Delight, Bursting with Beef'. Among the strict laws handed down by the Koran there is, I imagine, nothing that corresponds to our Trades Descriptions Act. What arrives is a pile of small toasted pitta bread sandwiches containing thin layers of beef and ham. I yearn for curry.

The sound for the concert is in the hands of three young Americans, very pleasant and cooperative. When we start to play, to an audience of around seven hundred, the usual drawbacks of open-air playing reveal themselves—with no buildings in the vicinity of the stage, there is nothing for the sound to bounce back off, and it seems very small and dry to us on stage. I dislike the fold-back monitors which they use to counteract this. Unless they are very carefully balanced and tuned, they throw a distorted sound back in your face. Reports from the front say that the sound is good, so I don't fuss.

The first half goes well, though without the aid of wild cheering and whistling that greeted us at Dubai. In the interval Tim King comes back to say, 'Don't be put off by the relatively subdued audience. They're loving it, but we're on uncertain ground so we're keeping a low profile.' In this they are no doubt assisted by the sight of several fully manned police cars constantly cruising past the main gates. As far as anyone on the concert committee knows, we are the first 'Western' band of any kind ever to perform so publicly in Saudi Arabia, where music plays no part in their culture. The oil company compounds out in the desert have had visiting groups, but that's not quite the same as blasting away alfresco in the middle of Jeddah. No one quite knows what the official view is, but they suspect that if the audience response is too riotous, the police will move in and put a stop to everything. Hence the decorous behaviour. By the end of the concert, however, inhibitions—and the police cars—vanish and everyone whoops and yells.

Afterwards, some of us go to a party in the top-storey flat of a German member of the concert committee. As we sit on the balcony eating take-away pizzas and surveying an incredibly quiet and peaceful panorama of Jeddah, I think 'So this is the trouble spot that has the whole world on tenterhooks!' Helmut's party (Alan Jackson refers to him as ' 'Elmet'—par for the course for someone who once thanked a West Country vicar for his hospitality after a concert with the words: 'Nice one, Vic!') rounds off a day that has raised our spirits.

Friday, 30 November 1979, Jeddah

Today being the Arab 'Sunday', we have a day off. We have an open invitation from several committee members to spend the day at the Red Sea Sailing Club, a few miles out of the city. This is one of several recreational facilities which the expatriate communities have won for themselves. Some of the band prefer to stay in the hotel, but several of us—John, Alan and Dave with a German called Walter, myself with Tim and Adrianne King and daughter Natasha—opt for whatever surprises the last day of the Red Sea Regatta might have in store.

Thirty minutes out of Jeddah in Tim's car, we dive off the main road and cross the sand to an enclosed compound on the sea shore. We go into a clubhouse and change for the beach, emerging on to a scene resembling a rather overdone parody of a Rubens painting. The strict Islamic law that forbids women to appear in public unless covered down to the wrists and ankles is in abeyance here, since the club is for Europeans only. The result is an explosion of liberated flesh which the flimsiest of bikinis make no serious effort to contain. Stalking out into this undulating landscape, I'm aware that I cut an odd figure. Tim King has warned us that on the Red Sea beach there are creatures—whether fish or insect I didn't take in—that lurk under the sand projecting a poisonous spear upwards which, if trodden on with a bare foot, will put one in hospital if not the mortuary. My sandals came adrift days ago and, having size thirteen feet, I can't just walk into a shop and replace them. So I have come to the beach in ordinary black shoes, all right when partly shrouded by trouser bottoms, but painfully conspicuous at the end of bare legs. However, I'm reassured by the sights around me that the prevailing mood is 'What the hell!' and stride forth unabashed.

It's a pleasant holiday atmosphere on the beach—we sit on rugs, sip soft drinks and watch the finals of the small-boat race. During a lull, Walter takes John and A.J. for a spin in a racing dinghy. A.J. returns ecstatic. 'Sailin' in the Red Sea—that's got to be good, 'asnit!' We have a salad lunch in the clubhouse, drinking something rather pleasant from bottles labelled 'Grape Juice'. Afterwards, in the interests of experience, I allow Tim to take me out in a craft which is only marginally larger than one of my shoes. Before we scud off into deep waters, he explains to me about 'tacking'. 'When I say "Get down!", crouch as low as you can in the boat—otherwise the boom will swing across and hit you.' Tim has not secured advancement in the diplomatic service for nothing. He is eminently unflappable, and when he first says 'Get down' it's in such a calm, everyday voice that I pay no attention. The boom is light aluminium, but even so it moves fast and can give you a fair whack on the side of the head. I get a few more clobbers before we're through as I'm not the shape to be furled quickly into a space the size of a small hip bath. I get back to the jetty bruised, drenched but exhilarated. The little boats skim along at a surprising speed when the wind catches them, and all the bumping and wind-lashing gingers up the senses. Before we leave, Tim officiates at the prize-giving, handing out trophies to Bill and Eileen, Gunther and Erika, Clive, Andy and Ray. In the midst of a tension-wracked Middle East, it's all gloriously mundane. Back to the hotel glowing with sun, brine and ozone for supper and early bed.

Saturday, 1 December 1979, Jeddah
Hot, dry day, spend the morning sunbathing and swimming at the British Embassy pool. The only snag about it is that it's a sweaty, 25-minute walk to and from the hotel, which undoes all the cooling-off effect at the end.

Today we have our first health crisis. John Barnes, having had two nasty-looking insect bites on his wrist, reveals red tracks extending up his arm, a clear sign of poisoning. We send him to the Embassy nurse, who in turn packs him off to a doctor in town. He returns with a bum punctured by a penicillin injection and strict instructions not to play tonight. They *think* they have intercepted septicaemia in time, but he has to go back at 4.15 for a check-up.

We're getting rather bored with the coffee-shop lunches at the Sands Hotel. The menu is very limited and far from exotic, considering we are in a land rich in colourful and aromatic spices. Toasted sandwiches, chicken in a basket and deep-fried plaice are the only alternative to interminable omelettes.

Jim McGrath and Ian Palmeter are due to come and pick us

up at the hotel at 4 o'clock to take us to the souk, reputed to be the largest and most picturesque in the Middle East. Ian doesn't turn up, so Bruce and I are left behind. It's just as well, as J.B. returns from the doctor's in very low spirits, having been told that he definitely can't play tonight and possibly not tomorrow either. It's not a complete disaster for the band, as we have a conventional Dixieland front-line left, with Bruce on clarinet. But I know how John feels. The deepest depression I have experienced in recent years was when I was prevented from going with the band to Prague because of one of my periodical bouts of nose-bleed. My nose doesn't just bleed, it bursts like a dam and has to be plugged with a yard-and-a-half of tightly-packed muslin. I sat at home looking like the Elephant Man and moping while the band flew off to Czechoslovakia with a substitute. You'd think we'd jump at the chance of a day or two off, but it doesn't work like that. Bruce, incidentally, is not broken-hearted at missing a trip to the souk. When he asked to be counted in, there was general surprise. Bruce buying presents for the folks at home? 'Never!' he said vehemently. 'Going to pinch money out of a blind man's bowl . . . probably pinch the bowl, too!'

Despite the depleted band, the concert goes well, with about the same number as last night. We learn that Ian's party, scheduled for tonight, is off—apparently his wife has just suffered a miscarriage, which explains why he seems on the point of releasing a bottled-up nervous breakdown.

Sunday, 2 December 1979, Jeddah
Another lazy day at the pool. John goes again to the doctor, returns with a clean bill of health. The tracking marks are still there, but they are receding, and he can play tonight. In the evening Helmut turns up to drive some of us to the souk. Here it's in a huge covered area, with an older part, uncovered, beyond. 'Moral police' are there to keep an eye on behaviour, and women showing too much leg or upper arm are liable to have the misdemeanour brought home to them with a whack on the shins with a stick carried for the purpose. But the stories of European wives having to shroud themselves from head to foot are exaggerated. Discretion and commonsense are the

watchwords. Dresses that extend to the mid-calf and have sleeves below the elbow are acceptable although, of course, the Arab women are heavily shrouded, sometimes with masks covering the face, sometimes totally hidden under layers of black veiling. Subdued they are not, however. At the counters and on the sidewalk they jostle and elbow like Rugby forwards, and it's a common sight to see a lordly head of the family stalking through the souk with a black Dalek trundling along ten paces in the rear nagging and bossing away from behind layers of impenetrable veiling. (When I mention this to one of the seasoned expatriates, he said it may just *sound* like nagging—most public conversations in Arabic sound like a flaming row.)

In an open space, a surprising sight—a young Arab woman sitting on some steps feeding a baby, the coffee-coloured breast highlighted against the black shroud. No 'moral police' descend on her with sticks flailing, no clucking chaperones huddle round to shield her from the public gaze. Later in the day, someone at the Embassy explains the contradiction to us. In Islamic religious culture, motherhood is sacred. In public a bare breast, in use as nature intended, symbolizes that motherhood, whereas a bare thigh, upper arm or even cheek represents an unambiguous challenge to chastity. I should add that interpretations of Islamic thoughts and customs come as cheaply as Christmas cracker mottoes here, and I take no responsibility if the foregoing is inaccurate. But at least it offers an explanation for the incongruous sight.

Less easy for the Western tourist to understand is the Saudi Arab's sensitivity to the prying camera lens. There are some staggering buildings in the old part of the souk, one in particular, built with wooden slats and crossbeams and lurching over the walkway with a rickety gracefulness, making the trigger finger itch. But cameras are not smiled upon here, and if you start snapping any of the more picturesque sights, it will be a passing Arab, not necessarily a policeman, who will knock the camera out of your hand. Here again, the hostility is difficult for Westerners to understand. The image that oil-rich Arabia wants to project is of an emergent, forward-looking, modern region hot on the heels of the world's most advanced and sophisticated countries. Antiquarian, olde worlde nostalgia has no part in this philosophy, nor does the tourism which it attracts. To us, photogenic old buildings, quaint donkey carts and elementary Bedouin implements might seem intriguing relics of Biblical times, but to the Arabs, even those still dressed in primeval garb, they are primitive aspects of a present from which they are urgently trying to escape. Certainly, ancient and modern are juxtaposed in a disconcerting way. Money-changers, for instance, sit on stools or on the pavement outside their booths, rapidly doing their sums on smart, expensive calculators. Indeed, it's useful to have a pocket Casio or Sinclair at the ready when buying anything. It makes the haggling more convincing.

The British in general, and myself in particular, are hopeless hagglers. It's the acting that's the stumbling block—the derisive shout of laughter when the first figure is quoted, the pretence that something that you've expressly gone into the shop to buy is a load of junk worth half the price at most, the walking away at regular intervals with the jaw jutting resolutely but the ears flapping for the inevitable recall for further bargaining. Trade union leaders no doubt find it all in a day's work, but I cave in with the first final offer.

For a country that shrouds its women in black, there's an extraordinary array of colourful and exotic clothes and fabrics in the souk, manufactured in India or China. The crocheted and embroidered blouses and sumptuous green or claret gowns with gold facings look magnificent in bulk in the stores here. I'm not sure how they'll 'travel', but buy a few things for the girls back home. The only other things I'm tempted by are the spices, especially frankincense and myrrh, so evocative of Scripture lessons at school. I daren't buy any because it would give away my touristic motives if I asked whether you eat it, smoke it or just wave it about, and what's more I have a suspicion that it might be the sort of stuff that permeates your clothes and luggage and leaves you smelling of cheap hair-oil for weeks. On the way back, where the old and newer markets join, we have to paddle round a foul-smelling morass where a sewer has overflowed. A whiff of frankincense would come in handy here.

Another good concert at full strength in the evening, then a formal reception at Tim King's house in the Embassy. We meet the new British ambassador, Sir James Craig, and sundry important diplomats and journalists, also a lady called Penny Arnot who is, they say, under threat of a flogging sentence for holding a drinks party at which a young English nurse, Helen Smith, died. Her husband, a doctor, is in prison at the moment for the same offence. The somewhat insecure atmosphere that we've felt in all the European gatherings in Saudi Arabia comes over strongly at this party. It manifests itself in the sharpness with which Tim turfs us out of the kitchen to which, with the musician's proclivity to find his own level we have naturally gravitated. He is right, of course—we are there as guests to mingle, not to retire from the fray to chat with the Indian staff and short-circuit the supply of food. To those who are put out by an unceremonious shooing out, I say, 'Forget about it—there are wheels within wheels out here. It's not like home.' They are lulled by this homespun wisdom, and we leave an hour or two later in good spirits.

As we walk into the hotel and pick up our keys, the Lebanese manager and his assistant behind the counter look knowing and say, 'I believe you have had an entertaining time.' This seems a common Arab ploy, to drop hints that one's every move is watched. I retire to bed and fall into an uneasy sleep, to be woken almost immediately by sounds of a riot in the corridor outside. The band has been overtaken by end-of-term euphoria. Machine-gun laughter ricochets round the corridor as A.J. pounds on Roy Williams's door, from which Roy emerges shouting 'Look here, my man . . .' in his best, and loudest, Lord De Vere voice. As I peer round my door, feeling like a headmaster interrupting a dormitory rag, John Barnes comes out of his room stark naked except for a half-heartedly deployed face towel. There is genuine panic in my voice as I hiss, 'For Christ's sake watch it, fellers—you're in *Jeddah*!!!' The reminder has its effect and they retire hastily, leaving me to spend a sleepless hour or two with the horrors over what might have happened—the complaint to the police, the sudden swoop, the instant incarceration in a dark and airless prison, the months of diplomatic efforts for our release, three hundred lashes in the public arena, deportation, then up before David Dimbleby on 'Panorama' . . .

Still horror-struck when I wake up—so are the guys when I remind them of last night's events. 'Oh, Christ!' seems to be the general view. There is a mix-up at the desk over the bills. We had the impression from Jim McGrath when we arrived that the hotel rooms were 370 Saudi Riyals less 15% discount. Today it transpires that the charge is actually 370 Riyals *plus* a 15% surcharge, which is waived for our benefit. It shouldn't make much material difference since the expenses allowance covers it with quite a bit to spare. But psychologically, near the end of a longish tour, it's disrupting, especially as some of the band, after some forward budgeting based on the original information, have not left themselves enough to pay their bill. The Egyptian British Council assistant, a nice, heavily-moustached man called Mahgdi, steps in and bales them out. Bruce is, needless to say, not one of those financially embarrassed, although he suffered a mortal blow a day or two ago when his Kuwait money, untouched and hoarded for several days, disappeared from a jacket imprudently left in his hotel room. The trouble with being a self-confessed—nay, self-boasted—miser is that disasters of this kind attract very little sympathy from spendthrift companions. When he came down into the foyer muttering, 'Thought they didn't steal here, thought they didn't steal here', the hilarity could not have been more callous had it been his trousers that had been pinched. Mick Pyne also had a much lesser amount taken on the same day. We asked around for advice about reporting it, and the answer was unanimous—'save your breath.'

Having extricated ourselves from the hotel, we are driven to the airport to fly to Amman. There's one stop at Medina, which with Mecca is one of the holy cities from which unbelievers are excluded. We off-load a few dozen pilgrims and are then bustled out again. A bearded British Council man meets us at Amman, and introduces himself as John Chapman. He gives out itineraries which tell us that, after a twenty-minute stop-off at the hotel for a check-in and wash, we leave by bus for the University of Yarmouk, ninety minutes' drive away, to do a short concert for the students. As our plane from Jeddah was exactly twenty minutes overdue we are late even before we start. John agrees to postpone the start for fifteen minutes, but we are still a bit travel-stained when we get on the small coach and drive off. Amman is built on seven hills, and its outskirts consist of a series of lumps and bumps completely covered in small, square dwellings. John explains that people who come into the city are allowed to put up a building on any flat surface they can find, and if the house survives for a period without dropping off into the valley, it will be supplied with electricity and services. Further out of the city, we pass a Palestinian refugee camp, a huge shanty city dating from the expulsion of Palestinian forces from Jordan in the early Seventies. With its broad, parallel 'streets' and rows of ramshackle shops it looks like Welwyn Garden City after the passage of a hurricane.

The bumpy trundle to Yarmouk takes all of the promised hour-and-a-half, and by the time we've unloaded the instruments we are forty-five minutes late for the concert. It's with some trepidation that we troop into a lecture room full to bursting point with vociferous students. As soon as we appear a huge cheer goes up and the place is clamorous with expectation as we set up on stage. John has told us that, as this is an extra-curricular show put in at the request of the University, we need do no more than forty-five minutes—especially, he adds, as they probably don't know anything about jazz and certainly know nothing about us except what they may have picked up from radio snippets announcing our tour. What, I am forced to wonder, are they all cheering? I am none the wiser when we start to play and an enormous swell of noise and movement greets the opening bars. We blow against a barrage of clapping, shouting and jostling, but there are friendly smiles everywhere and a pervading atmosphere of goodwill. At one point in the short concert, while Alan Jackson is playing a drum solo, a young man jumps on to the low platform and dances to and fro with lithe, athletic, hip-wiggling movements that make John Travolta look arthritic. After about thirty seconds he jumps down again to the wild applause of his fellow students. Somehow, the short episode is totally innocent of the boring exhibitionism which such invasions of the stage carry at home. The young man isn't drunk, nor does he outstay his welcome or barge into the instruments. It's an entirely spontaneous burst of genuine participation and adds to the overall feeling of warmth with which the whole show is bathed.

The wild enthusiasm is maintained right up until the last number. During one of the other solos towards the end, I nip offstage and suggest to John Chapman that *he* should tell them at the end that the show is over. It's pure funk—with this degree of tension and excitement I anticipate an outburst of disappointment and protest when it all ends abruptly. So we play a finale and I signal John on. He explains to an audience that has gone suddenly quiet and attentive that we have had a long journey and must return to Amman to rest before our big concert tomorrow. As he speaks, there are shouts of 'That's OK!' and 'Bravo!' from all over the hall, and the young people get up and begin to troop out, except for a small crowd that mills around as we pack up, picking up and examining the instruments and talking to us eagerly.

Had we been pop idols of their own age at the end of a three-hour concert, we could not have been received with more genuine warmth and enthusiasm. As they gather round and talk to us at the end, a young man comes over to me and introduces the only note of dissension. He pumps my hand and, in tones of ecstasy, cries, 'Sir, we have very much enjoyed your concert of Western music. But why no Beethoven?' I begin to explain that there are different kinds of Western music, but he will have none of it. 'No, sir, you should have played Beethoven's Fifth Symphony, but I do not complain. You are the king of music!'

It's been an extraordinary and exhilarating evening. The most remarkable aspect has been the *politeness* of the young and excitable crowd. No grumbles or boos at our lateness, no shouts of angry protest when John announced the end, and nothing but friendliness in the hubbub that accompanied the music. Discussing it afterwards, we agree that there was something almost frightening in the unanimity of the audience —it produced the sort of passionate crowd-feeling which, in other circumstances, could inspire them to burn down the University. But for us, it was nothing other than benevolent, and it took a meal with the staff, answering a lot of academic questions about jazz and eating lukewarm steak, peas and potatoes, to bring us down to earth.

One of the sights pointed out to us on the journey to Yarmouk was what remains of the Roman city of Jerash, whose pillars and colonnades can just be seen from the road. On the way back, still euphoric and encouraged by a full moon, we call on our Jordanian driver to pull off the road at the spot. He parks the bus and we spill out and clamber down to a wide Roman street lined with an avenue of pillars. It's a mad and magical feeling to stroll at midnight into the huge forum and sit around on the remains of stone seats taking in the weird moonlit scene. After a while I hear the furious barking of a dog somewhere in the hills and getting rapidly nearer. With rabies in mind, it seems a good moment to re-embark, and I set off ahead of the others for the bus. Half way up the track leading to the road, I look up and, in a vivid, heart-thumping moment of fantasy, see the figure of Christ, bearded and robed, silhouetted against the light sky. It's our driver, who has got impatient and has walked out on to a promontory to see where we have got to. It's been a pretty peculiar evening all round, and it's probably just as well that I am overcome by belated fatigue once back on the bus and doze the rest of the way back to the hotel.

Tuesday 4 December 1979, Amman
This morning the Jordan *Times* has a write-up of last night's concert at Yarmouk, headlined 'HUMPHREY LYTTELTON PUTS ON A ROUSING JAZZ SHOW'. It explains the good humour when we arrived late by saying that the 400-500 students and university staff 'had been entertaining each other by telling jokes at the microphones'. Later it reports that 'all the swinging jazz pieces were acclaimed by deafening clapping, whistles, shouting and the traditional Bedouin ululating call. The final number of the show, 'Fish Seller', was most wildly applauded by students clapping and shouting 'Eh-la!' During the number's percussion interlude, the enthusiastic students jumped on to the stage and began performing a traditional Bedouin dance . . . The rousing success of the concert produced what is, for Jordan, a very rare sight—after the show, a group of fans and autograph-hunters mobbed the players. Clearly, Humphrey Lyttelton is a musician who knows how to

reach his audience.' And vice versa.

I have to be up at 8.15 in order to go with John Chapman to Radio Jordan for a half-hour interview. Every regime in the Middle East seems to be in a jittery state and on the alert for sudden outbreaks of Islamic fundamentalism. We have to go through a security routine more appropriate to the Pentagon in its checking and counter-checking, but eventually get through to the studios and talk to a well-briefed interviewer who is well armed with my records and filters five tracks into the discussion. There's time for a quick coffee at the hotel before we are picked up to go to the University of Jordan in Amman for a short lunchtime concert similar to last night's at Yarmouk. The audience is smaller here, and it would be too much to expect a repetition of the wild scenes. But again there is the enthusiastic hubbub and friendly reception. Afterwards, there's another manifestation of the politeness which struck me last night. As we pack up, music starts up backstage— silvery guitar sounds from a distant corner. One of the students has brought a lute back and is strumming away to a group of friends in the shadows. Our immediate thoughts, conditioned by experience at home, are uncharitable. 'Here's someone trying to get in on the act—don't encourage him or he'll go on all day.' Remembering the diplomatic purpose behind our visit, one or two of us go over to listen. The young man is an adept player and the music has a tangy, flamenco-like verve. When he finishes the piece, he smiles at us and puts the instrument down. His delight when we ask him to play some more is a joy to see. This time a friend joins in, singing one of those minor-key Arab songs that seem to be searching rather uncertainly for a note substantial enough to land on. Again, the piece is very short and ends with an air of finality. With rallying cries coming from the bus outside, we apologise for having to leave. The young man with the lute waves away our regrets. 'No, no, thank you for listening. We enjoyed your music, thank you for listening to ours.'

Someone has the good idea of taking us straight from the university to the Palace of Culture where we are to play tonight, so that we can dump the instruments. When we get there, it's locked up, and though we shout, thump and yodel outside, no one comes to open up. A bad idea after all, so we go back to the hotel. An English girl journalist called Sara who, with a Chinese colleague, came to Yarmouk on the bus last night, is at the hotel and offers to be our guide this afternoon on a shopping-cum-sightseeing trip. After a sandwich lunch we drive off going first to one or two shops which she recommends. They are scattered in small clusters over the seven hills, usually near the big, open intersections where the main roads meet, so one gets little idea of a teeming city centre. After the concentrated hubbub of the souk in Jeddah, the souvenir shops here, with their rows of bronze pots and daggers and the ubiquitous olive-wood camels, strike us as rather wan and disappointing. The nicest things here are the boxes, necklaces and pendants made of mother-of-pearl, and I pick up a few to take home. I think Sara is a bit confused as to what we actually want, so she takes us down to the busy area around the Roman amphitheatre, which I suppose is the nearest thing to the old town centre. This is more like it—nothing so picturesque as a souk, but a fine jumble of hardware junk, hi-fi equipment and craft-shops. Across the way from all this commerce, taxis, buses and charabancs jostle noisily round the great steep-sided bowl of the amphitheatre. It ignores them with the taciturn aloofness of extreme age. Its tiers of seats soaring up to the open sky look splendid, but there's only time for a tantalizing scamper round the outside before we have to take a taxi back to the hotel.

The evening begins badly. Dressing after a shower, I suddenly notice that the gold ring which I bought in Kuwait is missing from my finger. It was a little loose, especially since we came to the cooler temperature of Amman, but surely not loose enough to have just dropped off in the street or taxi. I assume that all the flailing about getting in and out of shirts has dislodged it, so get down on hands and knees and search every inch of the wall-to-wall carpeted floor, moving all the furniture about. Nothing. Commonsense urges me to be philosophical. It has fallen off somewhere and is gone, so forget it. You have lived for fifty-eight years without wearing a ring, you can surely stagger through the next fifty-eight similarly unencumbered. People who are meant to wear rings don't lose them. You bought it with joke money anyway, so just lie down, have a rest before the show and think of something else. But this is ridiculous, I shout back at my distraught image in the bedroom mirror—things don't just disappear. The next minute I am clawing away at the fixed bed-head which comes away from the wall surprisingly easily for such a patently new fitting. Apart from a row of grinning nails, it reveals nothing.

There's something unsettling about losing things. Having put the room back together, I go down to the bus, feeling disgruntled and glum. The concert does nothing to cheer me up. The Palace of Culture is a huge place with the sort of vast open stage that induces agoraphobia. John Chapman estimates an audience of around eleven hundred. Since King Hussein, absent in Riyadh for a crisis conference of Arab rulers, is represented by his Minister of Culture, there is a certain amount of protocol to go through before the music starts, and I have to memorize an opening speech which John gives me, thanking the government for inviting us, the British Council for arranging things and the Minister for coming. There's nothing like the vibrant expectancy of Yarmouk, but we get a good ovation when we walk on and there's no reason to suppose that the show will not produce an exhilarating climax to the tour. No reason, that is, except for the presence of Jordanian TV, recording the whole show. We could have conquered the distraction of cameras gliding around the stage and peering into our faces. But as soon as we start to play, we realize that there is something seriously wrong with the sound. Bruce Turner's microphone is dead (Bruce is, of all of us, the most psychologically dependant on microphones, and it is *always* his that fails to work), and the piano and bass start loud and get steadily louder. It becomes clear that, while on stage our brains are being scrambled by noise, nothing very coherent or compact is getting across to the audience, whose applause is generous but short of ecstatic. All through the first half, we keep going off in turn during solos to shout up at the people in the control box above the stage, but they speak no English. John Chapman comes back to say that it's not too bad out in front, but that is little consolation when the din that we hear is driving every musical thought out of our heads.

By the interval I am gibbering. The TV producer is brought backstage to persuade me that the sound is perfect. John makes soothing noises, assuring me that the audience is loving every minute of it. I feel the desperation of a hospital patient being told that the pain that is bending him double doesn't exist. Just before we go on, a message comes back that, yes, they *have* found a fault in the sound circuit. What has been recorded for on TV has been fine, it's only in the hall that there has been distortion. Muttering a curse on sound men in general and all TV sound men in particular, I go back on to find that everything is, indeed, vastly improved. Unfortunately, our nerves are now shot. A.J., in particular, has sought refuge from frustration among the refreshments in the band-room and is not wholly in touch. In other circumstances, his climactic drum solo would have been hilarious. Always a master of light and shade, he takes things to extremes tonight, at one stage embarking on a long passage with both sticks pressed silently into the head of the snare-drum, only the rhythmic move-ments of his arms and shoulders revealing what musical thoughts are going on in his head. Then, instead of giving us our cue to come back in, he stops, carefully puts the sticks in their sling and stands up, arms raised towards the audience in a gesture of peace and benediction. He gets huge applause, and the concert ends with prolonged clapping and cheering. But it's been a nightmare to me.

Afterwards, we go to the home of British Council head Richard Long for a reception. While I am standing in line waiting to be presented to the Minister of Culture and his wife, the sound of hot harmonica-playing comes from another part of the room. The mixture of formal protocol and this outburst of free expression is disconcerting, and I'm relieved that, as far as I know, none of my colleagues plays the mouth-organ. Formalities over, I am mingling when someone brings over a distinguished-looking grey-haired man and introduces him as Mr So-and-so (a Turkish-sounding name), the Jordanian Director of Planning and Foreign Relations at the Department of Health. Without preamble he whips a mouth-organ out of the top pocket of his dinner-jacket and launches into 'I Got Rhythm', staring at me intently over his cupped hands. He plays quite well in a sort of Larry Adler fashion, but there's nothing more embarrassing than being played at, eyeball to eyeball, and I'm glad when he stops. In conversation it transpires that he is Armenian by birth and, apart from his political achievements, is renowned in Jordan as a hot mouth-organist. The evening has now taken on a totally surrealist character, and I am not in the least surprised when, our conversation having moved on to the current vogue for tap-dancing, he says, 'If I'd known you were interested, Mr Lyttelton, I would have brought my tap-shoes.' This must draw a whinnying noise out of me, because the people around assure me, when he has moved away, that he is a recognized authority on tap dancing and has written a book on it. How does he have time to cope with Health, Planning *and* Foreign Relations?

Back in the hotel, I am stripping off for final ablutions when something tinkles on to the tiled floor. It is my gold ring. Ever since I first noticed its disappearance it has been lodged smugly in a fold at the top of my underpants.

Wednesday, 5 December 1979, Amman
Leave the hotel at 9.30 for the airport. John Chapman shows us a write-up in the paper. It gives a glowing account of our performance, with special praise for our tonal finesse and overall balance. A.J.'s drum solo is singled out as a highspot, especially for its subtlety in the quiet passages—lost, says the reviewer, on some of the restless elements in the audience. So that's all right.

Sunday, 3 January 1982, Kuwait

Alarm call at 6.15. Day starts with a panic—I've hired an Avis
Ford Fiesta to go to Heathrow, and packed trumpet, suitcase,
bag with passport, travellers cheques etc. into the boot last
night so I wouldn't forget them. Discover this morning that I
don't know how the boot opens—a straightforward turn of
the key doesn't achieve anything. A day's supply of adrenalin is
expended before I discover the knack. Forty quid seems a lot
for the few hours that I have use of the car, but it's handy just
to dump it at Heathrow.

In the departure lounge we meet Sian Griffiths, from the
music department of the British Council—a tall, boyish-
looking lady out of the Joyce Grenfell box of soldiers, a fact of
which she must be aware, as her conversation frequently lapses
into Grenfellese. She is accompanying us this time, as
chaperone and also to visit the various British Council
outposts. On first impressions, a good trouper.

Flight is on a British Airways Tri-Star—good service
including free cocktails. Every time I fly on a jumbo, there's a
Walter Matthau movie. This time it's a boring film about
Women's Lib at the Supreme Court. Last time it was about
Glenda Jackson Lib in a hospital. I can't hear properly through
those Christmas cracker headphones, and get a headache
through pressing them into my ears. To borrow one of Bruce
Turner's conversational slogans, sleep's best. My in-flight
entertainment is restricted, too, by the fact that the comedy
audio channel is one that I present and therefore know by

heart, and a hefty portion of BA's house magazine *Highlife* is taken up by an article by me. Repressing a childish urge to wave magazine and headphones aloft shouting, 'That's me, that's me!' I succumb to the inevitable and sink into an in-flight stupor. They used to say that if you stood in Piccadilly for an hour you were bound to see someone you know. Nowadays you'd be lucky to see someone who speaks the same language, and the saying has been transferred to airports and aeroplanes. This time it's a family who came to our concert in Dubai in 1979, turned up again at an open-air do in Bath on Royal Wedding night, and now wave to us across the aisle of our Kuwait-bound jumbo. It's not that it's a small world, it's just that we travel around it on a very limited number of narrow rabbit-runs on which one is bound to meet acquaintances as frequently as in a village street. A week after we returned from our last Middle East tour, I stood behind a lady in the check-out queue at Waitrose in Whetstone who turned and said, 'We did enjoy your concert last week in Jeddah!'

Arrive in Kuwait at 7 p.m., met by British Council man Bruce Brown and by Tony Barlow, who is the manager of the Messila Beach Hotel where we are playing this time. They take us to the hotel, which is a sprawl of modern buildings encircled by a wall—a 'complex' is the correct jargon, and very apt too, since you need map and compass to find your way round it. We eat in the coffee shop, then retire to our huge bedrooms to watch TV. The choice is between in-house video movies and Kuwait TV, which is an odd mixture of Koranic sermons, prayer sessions, pop programmes and American imports like the 'Monte Carlo Show'. Once again, sleep's best.

Monday, 4 January 1982, Kuwait
Slept till 9.45. This morning we have a sound-check for our show in the ballroom tonight. The Italian sound man called Pietro goes to town on a cavernous 'nightclub' echo which we urgently nip in the bud. Transportation is much easier this time, since Sian has organized through the Council a solid fibreglass case for Dave Green's bass and a huge padded chest on castors which will take the drum kit, the sensitive baritone saxophone, all my home-made music-stands (a brilliant inven-

tion of mine, made of three-ply card and cut out in one piece which is then bent into shape—light as a feather), and my trumpet.

Lunch off a delicious local fish called *hamour* here, known in other parts of the world as grouper. Could have stuffed myself silly on the magnificently laid-out buffet, but had a feeling that I might swim this afternoon—there are two or three swimming pools secreted around the complex. The weather looks nice from indoors, but outside there's an icy breeze which rules out lying in the patchy sun, let alone swimming. Indoors, things are rough, too, with an old Stewart Grainger movie on TV. But there are odd jobs—sorting out the music for the concert, diary-writing, showering—to keep me busy. By 6.30 I'm hungry again, so walk across to the Coffee Shop for a steak smothered in ersatz Bearnaise sauce.

Having eaten, I meet the others to go to a brief drinks party at Tony Barlow's house. Sian has directions but isn't sure if their starting-point is inside or outside the hotel perimeter. She plumps for the latter and leads us round to a dusty road leading nowhere, where we are set upon by a large and ferocious dog. We turn back and retreat with the studied, clenched gait of persons who expect their rumps to be punctured by rabid teeth at any moment. We find the house inside the walls, and join a party at which I find it hard to concentrate on conversation. I'm never conscious of nerves before a concert, and reject the old theatrical myth that one can't give of one's best without enduring butterflies. I'm only really scared when I'm not sure what's going to happen—a 'special' show with guests, perhaps, or one in unpredictable surroundings—and then the butterflies have played havoc with my breathing and I've given of my worst. But I do find myself becoming abstracted and vague an hour or so before playing and prefer to be at the venue warming up, fiddling about with the instruments or just staring at the wall.

It's an informal show tonight, with the audience spread among tables and dining while we play. It's largely an expatriate crowd, though there are more native white dish-dashers than we had two years ago at the Marriott. During our first set, a group of Arabs come in wearing the red and white checked headscarves identifying them as Saudi Arabs from

101

over the border. They sit near the stage on our left, stashing several clanking plastic bags under the table. During someone else's solo spot I leave the stage and have a breather out of sight of most of the audience. One of the party waves me over. 'Are you in the music group?' he asks in an accent rattling with throaty aspirates and rolling r's. When I nod, he goes on, 'Then what are you doing behind the stage—praying?' White teeth flash in a gusty laugh, and from then on, whenever I catch his eye from the stage, I get a conspiratorial grin.

Tuesday, 5 January 1982, Kuwait
Cloudy today with rain about. Get up around 10 but take my time dressing as we have nothing to do this morning. Picked up at 1 o'clock by a stocky, dignified British Embassy driver whom I remember from last time as being the double of Geraldo's erstwhile guitarist Ivor Mairants. Everybody looks like somebody else—there aren't many original faces around. En route to our lunch date with the Ambassador, he tells me that he has been with the Embassy twenty-five years. The imminent prospect of a gold watch and testimonial has no restraining effect on his driving—we hurtle along at 80 m.p.h., braking at roundabouts with a force that threatens to catapult everyone into the minibus's front seat.

John Cambridge is still in residence as Ambassador, much thinner now after a severe illness but just as sprightly and hospitable. The lunch is a replica of our last visit—stand-up drinks, queue along the buffet, disperse to tables to eat, short mill-about afterwards. Food rather more ordinary this time—a new chef, or Thatcherite spending cuts making their distant presence felt? Her Minister of State for Transport is among the gathering, here on an official visit. We are introduced—his name is Kenneth Clark (the Creator's lack of inventiveness with regard to human faces is matched by man's limited imagination over names) and he turns out to be a jazz fan. Blond, chubby-faced and unpompous, he looks a bright hope. Well, a genuinely hip Prime Minister wouldn't be bad—Harold Wilson tried, but there was a square underneath.

At the concert last night we met up again with Carl Robert, who got us our dishdashers when we were in Kuwait last time.

102

In some sort of group aberration we all got his name wrong, but he stood up well to being greeted by us, one at a time, as 'Max'. He and his wife Jean invited us over after our Embassy visit today, as his flat is not far away. When we get there, we find that Jean, not knowing that it was a lunch with the Ambassador, has prepared a huge spread. Luckily, her vegetable samosas, spinach and garlic tarts etc. are so appetizing that we just keep on eating. Bloated, those of us already bitten by the spending bug go with the Roberts family to the Al-Kabir souk, a new, modern hyper-souk thrown up since our trip two years ago and, according to Carl, threatening to collapse just as quickly. Daughter Joan is a good haggler and we stock up with gold and hi-fi equipment. The former is more expensive than last time due to a rise in the world price, but a solid, 21-carat bracelet is still a good buy at the equivalent of £60, and a £100 Sony pocket cassette recorder can also be got for around £60 after a bit of pantomime.

The concert tonight is a repeat of last night, but with an even larger crowd. Again, dishdashers are in a minority, but informed opinion is that the predominantly European dress is misleading, as Kuwait's educational and commercial establishments are full of Egyptians, Iraquis, Syrians and the like, and they are well represented in the crowd.

Wednesday, 6 January 1982, Kuwait
Re yesterday's entry, why am I so keen to persuade myself that our audiences are not just homesick Britishers and Europeans? I suppose it's natural not to want to come all this way just to play for exiles from the Humphrey Lyttelton Club of the Fifties, and the 'Jazz Ambassador' bit does give all this schlapping about an extra dimension. But in the end, an audience is an audience . . .

Another good sleep, broken only by a massive thunderstorm at about 7 a.m. It cleared the air and today is fine and warm. Had an omelette and croissants at the Coffee Shop at 11.30, then we are taken at 12 to the Embassy Club at the invitation of the amiable double act, Iraqui Nuri Alvarez and Pakistani Sarwah (known in Arabic as Siru) whom we met here last time. Drank beer in pub atmosphere for two hours. Mr Siru promises to get me some cassettes of Arabic music, about which I learnt very little last time. I ask him especially for examples of Kuwaiti music, which has an African percussive element that brings it closer to jazz than most of the familiar minor key wailing.

After an inactive afternoon we go to the TTI Theatre at the Telecommunications Centre to do our concert. Not a sell-out as it was last time, but they say that the expatriate community is a trifle jaded after all the Christmas entertainment. Carl Robert, who still works with Kuwait Television, brings along a video camera and films the whole show from about nine rows back. He comes back at the end rubbing a cramped shoulder and expressing doubts about the outcome, as the stage lighting is dim by TV standards and he took the sound on the machine's own microphone.

After the show, we are all invited to a party at the home of Mr Twiggers, the administrator of the TTI place. He remembers me telling him at a reception last time we were here that we hadn't met very many Kuwaitis, so he has assembled a roomful of them, including a band—four or five drums of assorted sizes and a lute (the penny has finally dropped on this trip that the word 'lute' derives directly from the Arab name for the instrument, 'el oud'). When the delicious and sumptuous buffet is disposed of, there is a full-blown musical soirée. In accordance with Arab custom the Kuwaiti attendance is all male—that's the reason, someone explains, why Bedouin dancing is so extraordinarily camp, with effeminate hip-swaying and eye-rolling. Since women take no part in music or dancing (the famous female singers and, of course, belly dancers, are from Egypt, the Lebanon and Turkey, where things are different), Bedouin male dancing must imitate the female role. To my horror, I am singled out by a group of Kuwaitis to receive a lesson in the subject. Someone borrows a spare dishdasher, which is draped over me and surmounted by the head-dress assembly. Bursting out of this gear, which is five sizes too small, I am led on to the 'dance floor' by a plump and shining young man called Khaled and encouraged to shake a hip. They have a technique of finger-snapping which contributes occasional pistol-cracks to the percussive music—he tries to teach me, but it nearly breaks my fingers and achieves no more than a damp 'flip'. Anyone from home witnessing the scene might fairly have taken it as an exercise in humiliation, the baiting of a village idiot. But it's quite clearly a friendly and complimentary gesture, so I fling myself into the routine with abandon. But one can take the ambassador bit too far.

The music is fascinating. There is no harmony—the singer intones a teetering melody line which the lute follows in unison but with florid decoration, while the drums play a polyrhythmic accompaniment that is sometimes purely African in its complexity, but quite often has a familiar Latin American *habanera* thread for the Westerner to hang on to. Practically all the songs sound to us in a minor key, but it's probably more accurate to relate them to the minor-sounding modes (Dorian or Phrygian), with quartertones scattered about for good measure. There's another element of audience participation apart from the finger-cracking. At a given point the people sitting around begin to clap, on the off-beat at first and then increasing the beats until, clapping alternately and as accurately as castanets, they achieve the rattle of machine-gun fire. Mysteries abound—what signal do they get from the leader of the musicians to start, how is it decided spontaneously who will take the on-beat and who the off, and how do they know when it's time to stop? Apparently, this style of music is peculiar to Kuwait and much of it is of maritime origin, i.e. sailors' and fishermen's songs. Towards the end of the evening, John Barnes and Mike Paxton, our drummer on this trip, sit in with the band on borrowed drums but do little to show that they've got the hang of it. Someone points out the democratic nature of this amateur group of musicians—one drummer is the head of a huge oil concern, the other a cleaner at the University.

At the end of the night it's a dishevelled band that returns to the hotel. Roy Williams says that, passing the kitchen door to pick up his jacket, he hears our hostess saying 'Frankly, I think they're all a lot of poofs.' We don't know if she is referring to the hip-swaying Kuwaiti dancers or us. She has had a hard night. For most of the time her kitchen has been crowded with people—the English (not only our lot) attacking the drink supply at source, the Kuwaiti musicians tuning their drums by warming them in front of her oven. She must have been glad to see the back of us.

Thursday, 7 January 1982, Kuwait
Tonight we have another 'lecture' at the Mousetrap Theatre, on the lines of the one arranged by John Munby last time. This time, we take the instruments in the morning, do a quick sound check (no problem as there is only one microphone), and then are collected by the redoubtable Juanita Monteiro for lunch at her new house, which has risen from the sands next door to her brother's place where we were entertained last time. All around, new residences are going up or coming down. It's hard to tell which, because the naked plaster and timbering of the new buildings is scrappy and full of holes. Juanita's living-room is a positive Indo-Catholic Aladdin's cave, with glass chandeliers, gilt filigree decoration, engraved brass trays and table-tops, painted Madonnas and, pinned to the wall, a pennant inscribed God Bless This House. When she rang through with the invitation, she asked if we would bring our instruments to surprise her sick mother with a serenade outside her bedroom door. I can think of no quicker way to propel the poor lady into whatever next world she may be called, and am therefore relieved to be able to say that, alas, the instruments are all under lock and key at the Mousetrap. Once again J. provides a superb Indian meal in pleasant company, her brother Joe calling in while we are eating.

This evening, preparing to go on at the Mousetrap, we have a surprise visit from Edward Heath, who is in Kuwait for talks associated with the Brandt Commission. The British Council has sent him an invitation as a matter of courtesy and he turns up, to the obvious concern of his tour organizers, who have to get him to a dinner later on. He walks straight into the band-room to say 'Hello'. I was introduced to him at a *Punch* lunch when he was Prime Minister, but we exchanged few words and this visit can only have arisen from a thoughtful desire on his part to encourage the British Council's activities —and some fellow-musicians in the process. His politics are not mine, and many times I have ground my teeth to dust listening to his Prime Ministerial speeches. But contrary to the media image of an embittered Achilles sulking in his tent, he seems to present nowadays a far jollier, less frosty front, with a nice line in self-deprecatory humour. He tells us how he was serenaded over breakfast this morning by a Filipino band 'in pyjamas—I like breakfast to myself, don't you? I always hate working breakfasts with colleagues—not that they happen very often these days.' He says he'll have to leave the concert after fifteen minutes or so 'to go to this bloody dinner', but in the event hangs on for about half an hour, to the manifest consternation of his minders. Afterwards, even Bruce Turner the Stalinist was heard to say, 'Nice chap, nice chap.'

I ad-lib the whole lecture as before, and it goes well. Afterwards, there's a reception at the home of British Council chief Tom White and his French wife, Gabrielle. A good sprinkling of Arab functionaries there, including a small man with jet black eyebrows and moustache and a deep, King Hussein voice who says to me several times, 'I *wish* you like Kuwait.' The bass intonation sounds so sad and regretful that I am on the point of saying, 'Oh, but I *do*, I *do!*' when I realize that he means to say 'I hope . . .' Sit-down meal for a change— I am next to Mr Rajabi, the Arab husband of the English lady who runs the Mousetrap Theatre—he founded the English-Speaking School. Very informative, and with a sharp 'English' sense of humour. While we're talking about Kuwaiti music, jazz etc. I find myself thinking what a large part clothing plays in our perception of each other. If the BBC motto were amended from 'Nation shall speak unto nation' to 'Trousers shall speak unto nightgown, belt shall speak unto braces . . .' it would give a better idea of the job to be done. Here I am, finding myself surprised at holding an easy, relaxed and mutually-comprehending conversation with someone whom I had assumed would be different, awkward and alien, just because I am wearing collar, tie and jacket while he is in robe and head-dress. We might as well be wearing lapel-tags saying 'WILY ARAB' and 'BUTTONED-UP ENGLISHMAN' . . .

Friday, 8 January 1982, Bahrain
Up at 7 o'clock, assembled at 8 to drive to the airport. The

flight doesn't leave till mid-morning, but Bruce Brown anticipates problems with the elephantine bass case and flight box. He is right. When we present them to be checked in, the men at the desk shake their heads firmly—they cannot accept them. Sian is perturbed, but Bruce Brown says to me, 'Don't worry—they'll take them in the end, but we have to go through the procedure.' The 'procedure' consists of applying to escalating layers of authority, with a blank refusal every time until a top man, the director of the airport himself, comes down, looks at the offending cargo, nods silently and walks away. We are involved in another potential crisis regarding our stint in Saudi Arabia. Checking our passport visas for the Kuwait visit, Bruce Brown has discovered, just by chance, that some of the Saudi visas expire several days before we are due to go there. It seems that a clerk at the Saudi Embassy in London has, either inadvertently or with cussedness aforethought, dated the visas *for one month from the date of application*, which was some time early in December. Telexes have been sent ahead to Bahrain to try and sort it out.

Arriving in Bahrain ourselves, we are met by the British Council representative, a middle-aged, military-looking gent (with the sprawling name of Henry Bryce Bending. We assume it's double-barrelled, but he says 'Call me Bryce.' He is accompanied by his assistant, Roy Kannemeyer (from South Africa) and Arab driver-cum-Mr Fixit, Abbas, who wears European dress and probably hails, like the other 'local' council workers, from Egypt. It is Abbas who will have the job of trying to sort out our visas for Saudi Arabia.

Check in at the Sheraton Hotel, where we are to play and stay. Disaffection in some quarters over the expenses deal, largely due to a somewhat brusque and insensitive note to each of us from the management outlining our 'entitlements'. We are on full board here, and some tender sensibilities are ruffled by the curt list of what we may, and more especially may NOT charge to the hotel. I have to point out that it's obviously a standard letter and you can't expect that to observe diplomatic niceties.

After the late night yesterday and early start this morning, everyone is bleary with fatigue. John Barnes and I decide to accept Roy Kannemeyer's invitation to a look around the island and hospitality at his place, on the grounds that if we crash into a deep sleep at five in the evening, it will throw our whole routine out for days. We go to the British Council Offices to pick up his car. It won't start, so transfer to a B.C. car, which won't start either. Eventually we get going, make a rapid tour of the island, then end up in his flat listening to jazz records and nibbling cashew nuts. Having formerly lived in Hounslow he knows all about the British jazz scene and we spend an enjoyable couple of hours nattering until fatigue finally engulfs us. Back to hotel around eight, where I ward off sleep for an hour or two more with a bath and a dud Marlon Brando/David Niven movie on the in-house circuit.

Saturday, 9 January 1982, Bahrain
Up at 8.30, having slept through since 11 o'clock last night. Postscript on yesterday's arrival at Bahrain Airport. Having come through customs and out on to the forecourt to load the transport, we discover that Bruce Turner is missing. It's not an unusual occurrence for him to disappear from view at crucial moments, so we pay little attention until it's time to pile into the minibus and leave for the hotel. Then search parties are sent in all directions, to see if he has been hung up in customs or has taken a wrong turning. Just as we are beginning to think that this is one of those Missing Persons mysteries that one reads about, a taxi pulls up outside and Bruce gets out and, with the expression of someone having a tooth pulled without anaesthetic, hands over money to the driver. It turns out that he was separated from us, went out of a different exit, mistook an importuning taxi driver to be our official transport, got into the cab and was whisked into the centre of town, where he managed to convey to a totally bewildered cabbie that he wanted to go straight back to the airport. Since it cost him money, we take this to be a genuine, rather than staged, aberration.

Go out shopping with John Barnes in the morning, trying unsuccessfully to get clarinet reeds. We find a well-equipped music shop, but all the reeds are too soft. One of the secrets of this kind of touring from one big hotel to another is to stock up with soft drinks, biscuits and other nibbles outside so that one doesn't have even to break the seal on the ludicrously expensive mini-bars in the hotel rooms. There a bag of KP nuts and two Cokes will knock a large hole in a fiver. So we buy fruit juices, cheese and biscuits in a self-service store. At noon, go out to the swimming pool, where the rest of the band are well advanced into the first sunbathing of the trip, already turning lobster pink. The sun is warm—about 75 degrees—but the water is numbing. Mad dogs, we know, have hydrophobia, but Englishmen leap into the midday pool whatever the temperature, and we didn't let the old country down.

Going back into the hotel, we meet Bryce Bending in the foyer, who has come to tell us that a TV session arranged for this afternoon has had to be postponed until tomorrow because the studio isn't ready. He also tells us that our Saudi Arabian visit is off, the authorities there having returned a Telex message saying that there is no way the visas can be corrected in time—which, literally translated, means that they have no intention of doing it. Remembering the hassles at the airport over our heavy baggage, I suspend all thought on the matter. It could all be different in the morning. The Sheraton buffet lunch is an invitation to instant cardiac arrest. Laid out on a huge raised altar in the middle of the dining-room, it is a veritable mountain of food, hot and cold, with lobster, smoked salmon and quails by no means the most spectacular offerings. The band, some still smarting from the management's stern exposition of our 'entitlements', take one look at it, assume that it will mop up their total allowance in one go, and retire to the snack restaurant down below. A closer look at the instructions would have told them that, for a set price that exactly matches our entitlement, they could swarm at will like locusts over the gastronomic mound and strip it down to the woodwork. Sian is calm about Saudi Arabia, says that wheels are still turning. I spend the afternoon stretched out like a gorged python on the bed, getting up in time to go with the others to a recommended emporium called the Nip In Liquor Store to further thwart the mini-bar. Alcoholic sales are allowed in Bahrain, but only in these special stores which are discreetly located away from the centre of town.

We play tonight in the hotel ballroom, to a largely expatriate audience. The atmosphere is quiet at first—the

110

room is one of those huge, ocean liner affairs, and I have a feeling that the sound isn't reaching every corner. A large bespectacled Englishman at a table on our right decides to take it upon himself to jolly things up, and starts some benign heckling in a booming voice. In my announcements I sometimes refer to the band sardonically as 'The Orchestra', which prompts him to bellow at one point, 'Mr Lyttelton, can you tell us exactly when a band becomes an orchestra?' It's clear as we go on that he is one of the Nip In Store's most loyal customers. Hearing me refer to the 'front line of the band', he comes across, commandeers a microphone and makes a speech about farting and the superior noise emanating from 'the back end of the band'. I thank him for raising the cultural tone and leave it to his manifestly embarrassed wife and friends to shut him up, which they do successfully. Everything warms up slowly but surely by the end, and a lot of people convey their intention to come again tomorrow. Finish the night off with a meal with Roy Kannemeyer and two Irish ladies in the snack restaurant.

Sunday, 10 January 1982, Bahrain
Nothing to do this morning, don't even bother to bestir myself for breakfast, but eat my own provisions in the room. The postponed TV show is on this afternoon. Bryce and Abbas pick us up to take us to the studio. We note that the British Council chief drives an old rattler, the driver-cum-fixer a sleek American limousine. They say he has a car business on the side. The studio is surrounded by heavy security, a sequel to the attempted coup by fundamentalists that was discovered and thwarted a few months ago. The locals refer to it as the Problem, in the way the Irish talk about the Troubles.

Inside we meet a lady, introduced as Miss Ziyani, who is said to be a famous TV director in Bahrain. In leather trousers and with long black hair, she looks decidedly slinky. She was trained in the United States and has a strong American accent to show for it. Why is it that an American accent superimposed on broken English spells bullshit? We have arrived at 2.45 p.m. to find the studio empty. It is only just finished, hence the postponement from yesterday. There is an expensive-looking

111

Variations on a theme...

composite floor as smooth as untrodden snow, and it is Mike Paxton who points out that if he drives the spurs of his drum kit into it, it will probably do thousands of pounds' worth of damage, a belief confirmed by Miss Ziyani with a look of horror. Men fall on the drums and start binding the spurs with plastic tape, a useless exercise. Someone is sent to find a piece of rug or matting on which the kit can be set up. Mick Pyne goes to the piano to try it out and finds it locked. Everyone in sight is asked who has the key, and it turns out to be someone who is off for the afternoon. A car has to be sent into Bahrain to track him down. Meanwhile Arab studio hands arrive with a huge Persian carpet the size of a squash court for the drums. They unroll it, and Mike prepares to set up his drums but is waved away. First a man must sweep it, which he does with a broom, sending up clouds of dust.

An hour goes by before the search party returns with the piano key. 'I guess we have to hurry,' says Miss Ziyani, heedless of the fact that there are still no microphones set up. We break again to wait for them. At 4 o'clock, the sound men return, with what appear to be newly-purchased microphones in boxes marked Amateur Sound Kit. We have to be finished by 4.45 at the latest, so once the amateur kit is assembled, we reel off six numbers straight to camera without rehearsal or sound check. Sian, who watches it all on the control room monitors, reports that both sound and shots are chaotic, and that every time a camera alights out of focus on the wrong musician or has its view blocked by another camera in transit, Miss Ziyani says 'Whoops!'

As soon as we finish, the band other than myself are rushed by car to the Bahrain souk to have mug-shots taken by the owner of the only polaroid camera in the city. The photos are needed for the application for fresh Saudi Arabian visas. Thanks to the coincidental arrival in Bahrain of the Saudi Arabian Ambassador for a goodwill visit to his British counterpart, it now seems as if the visa muddle *can* be resolved. After all this, a well-attended and headily-successful concert back at the hotel seems an anticlimax.

Monday, 11 January 1982, Doha
We fly out at 1.10 p.m. for Qatar, having left the hotel at

11 o'clock. The short journeys in this part of the world emphasize the truth that in any door-to-door journey by air, less than a third of the travelling time is actually in the air. We go through the new familiar pantomime over the heavy baggage, all the way from the first categorical refusal to the eventual cursory acceptance.

We are met at Doha Airport by Clive Bruton from the British Council, who hands out itineraries for the thirty-six hour stay. We shall be quite busy here—there's an official reception chez Clive and Carol Bruton tonight, and tomorrow morning, a one-hour concert for school children prior to the full evening concert. We are staying at the monolithic Ramada Hotel which is far from the town itself. There's the ubiquitous Coffee Shop for meals and a small pool for relaxation when time permits. We meet the hotel manager, John Murphy, who delegates his assistant, Terry Eisner, to show us the ballroom where we are to play tomorrow. I opt for a set-up of tables and chairs rather than serried ranks of seats.

Good party tonight at the Brutons'. We are presented to a VIP in full Arab gear who, as Director of the Department of Culture, has had a big say in facilitating our appearance here. His name is Mr Mosa—small, bespectacled and with dark, reticent eyes. He's not a great conversationalist and party talk is heavy going. But when something tickles him, his sombre face lights up surprisingly with a gleaming smile. His wife is Egyptian, and on his frequent visits to Cairo he has picked up a full repertoire of rather long-winded jokes about President Sadat which are in circulation there. For example, a 'long arm' in Egypt denotes a thief. After Sadat's assassination, the new President Mubarak goes to see the widow, who offers him one of Sadat's many imposing uniforms. Mubarak says 'Thank you, but it doesn't fit—the sleeve is too long.' 'Never mind,' says Mrs Sadat, 'it will soon fit you, too.' Having the conventional Western notion of Sadat as a Good Guy, I find myself being slightly shocked by this succession of parables depicting him as a crook. But I've left it too late in life to become a student of Arab politics.

Tuesday, 12 January 1983, Doha

Mindful of the long day ahead, I left the party at midnight, the rest of the band staying on. Apparently things warmed up considerably, judging by the balloon-like swelling round John Barne's ankle this morning. You can always tell when J.B. is getting into the spirit of things. The eyes start to blink, teeth like a row of tank-obstacles are bared in an eager grin, the beard juts, the hands clasp and unclasp each other and one knee starts to drive like a piston. All the signs point to an impending burst of Stanley Holloway and Rob Wilton monologues. Last night, when these were expended, he went on to demonstrate to the official from the Department of Culture the technique of Will Gaines, the black American tap-dancing wizard who was discovered some time ago working as a housepainter in Rotherham, England. Will has the fastest feet in the Western Hemisphere. J.B. has not, and they got entangled and brought him down, badly twisting his ankle in the process.

An assortment of cars arrive at the Ramada Hotel at 9.30 to take us to the children's concert this morning. The Doha Players Theatre is a squat white building on the sandy outskirts, founded and run by the English-speaking community for education and entertainment. I have, lodged in my memory, a routine for talking about jazz to children put together some years ago for a couple of schools lectures. While we're setting up and having a cup of tea, I collect together sundry props from the Theatre kitchen—a large tin teapot, some empty tins and a Coca Cola bottle. When we're ready, about four hundred children of all nationalities and colours troop in. We start with a short number, then I go through all the instruments, explaining how we get sounds out of them. When it comes to the brass instruments I get them all making the buzzing noise into imaginary mouthpieces. Four hundred children blowing raspberries sounds quite impressive. With the teapot I show how a tune can be got out of any metal object that involves tubing, and the tins and bottles demonstrate the idiosyncratic sounds that jazz players produce. Then we go on to build a conventional 'Dixieland' ensemble on the theme of 'Jingle Bells', working up to a jam session in which they all join in. Finally, a resumé of jazz origins leads to a march around the stage to 'High Society'. In the middle of this, a storm of whoops and giggles breaks out. I have forgotten about John's bad ankle, and the sight of him hobbling along painfully in the rear, baritone sax aloft, breaks the place up. John, the kindest and most congenial of men, hasn't a drop of false dignity in him, and he comes off, beard jutting with glee at the sensation he has caused. Given half a chance, he would have laid a monologue on them.

The hotel transport that brought us here has dismissed itself by the time we finish, so we get lifts back to the hotel on a motley fleet of cars and lorries. Lunch in the buffet, then a brief sit by the pool for me before an assistant manager of the hotel arrives to take some of us on a sightseeing trip to the Doha museum (we have to see *something* in Doha!). John Murphy has kindly put the hotel Cadillac at our disposal and his assistant, a plump Tunisian called Moncef, is clearly out to do the guide bit in style. The museum is in the grounds of what must once have been a royal Palace. There are rooms showing all aspects of Bedouin life, and once again, we come across the curious Arab ambivalence about the past. Wherever old implements, musical instruments and impedimenta are displayed, there are notices everywhere forbidding the taking of photographs. But it's not all antiquarian stuff. In one section there are detailed maps, diagrams and models of the geology of the Gulf, with special reference, of course, to oil. Most fascinating is a sort of well into which one peers to watch the geographical history of the area unfold in fast motion on a circular screen below. Like the oil bubbles in a trendy table lamp, seas expand and recede and land-masses collide, merge and recoil.

Elsewhere there's a fine aquarium showing the local marine life. I look for a *hamour* or grouper to see what the noble-tasting creature looks like before it's consigned to the pot, but they go in for stranger and, it has to be said, extraordinarily ugly local inhabitants. The Starry Pufferfish may sound glamorous, but it looks like a grey thug in a stocking-mask about to rob a subterranean bank. True, the Butterfly and Angel Fish have a certain glamour, but a glance at the catalogue suggests a pretty dangerous and unsavoury underworld below the waves. I wouldn't like to venture un-accompanied among the community of Snappers, Sweetlips,

Scavengers, Silver Biddies, Porgies, Wrasses, Flutemouths, Clownfishes, Gobies, Blennies, Puffers, Triggerfishes and Grunts. (Travelling with a crew of itinerant musicians one encounters enough Peppered Grunts in the early morning without wanting to seek them out under water!) Even the tasty *hamour*, which I eventually come across, turns out to be a 'large-mouthed, voracious, unspecified carnivore' that grows to over two metres in length and, at this size, will take an unwary diver's leg off at the knee. Outside in a quiet harbour there are ancient wooden dhows preserved. Moncef corrects my ignorant pronunciation—it's not 'dow' to rhyme with 'cow', but nearer to 'dough' or 'doh' in the tonic-solfa scale. But it must be articulated, as that sneaky 'h' demands, with an outrush of air and a sort of squeak at the end, as if one has been hit in the midriff by a heavyweight. Whack . . . 'Dhhhh-oh-we!!'

While we're looking round the aquarium, Moncef slips away, then comes back to say that he has arranged an audience for us with the head of the Museum. He is a small, venerable Egyptian, wrinkled and brown as a walnut, who, Moncef tells us beforehand, is a distinguished Arabist, writer and journalist well known throughout the Gulf. He greets us with a fusillade of 'Marhabas' and, sitting like schoolboys in the head's office on wall seats across the room from his huge desk, we talk of this and that. A man comes in with a tray of Arab coffee, a bitter concoction of white coffee beans and cardamom seed. We learn that there is protocol attached to such coffee drinking. It is rude to decline a first refill, greedy and uncouth to accept a second or third. So when the man first comes round, you hold your cup out steadily to be recharged. Second time round, you hold it out again but wobble it with a shake of the wrist to indicate that you have finished. At the end of our audience, the Curator gives us each a tiny, rough glass phial containing Arab perfume. Even corked up it gives off an aroma sweet and heavy enough to fell a bison. I find myself wondering, as I accept it with gracious thanks, how I'm going to take it home. It's a nice memento, after all, but if one drop leaks in my suitcase it's the bonfire for my shirts and underwear.

Back at the hotel, I do a radio interview with a young man called Malcolm Taylor, who turns out to be the nephew of my first trombonist, Harry Brown, who came to me from George Webb's Dixielanders in 1948.

The concert in the evening is a great success. Mr Mosa and his wife are there and quite a few berobed Arabs. As a matter of courtesy I start with the 'marhaba . . . masa' al-kher . . . ahlan wa sahlan' routine that I learnt on the last trip, and an uncouth British voice shouts, 'Talk bloody English!' Talking to Clive Bruton afterwards, he says that this sort of resistance by British expatriates to any movement towards the Arabs and Arab culture is the British Council's biggest problem. In the industrial field the aim seems to be to get here, make as much money as possible in the shortest possible time and clear out, shaking the sands of Arabia off the feet.

Wednesday, 13 January 1982, Abu Dhabi

These starts get earlier and earlier. Up at 5.30 this morning—the flight's not till 8.15 but we have to be prepared for the lengthy negotiations to get the baggage on. We cross a further dateline en route and alter our watches to four instead of three hours ahead of British time, arriving at 10 a.m. local time. Another Clive meets us, this time Clive Mogford, the British Council representative—on first sight a conventional Foreign Service type with collar, tie and jacket and a big moustache. He is called on early to exert diplomatic pressure, as the customs people, going through my hand baggage, come upon the video of our Kuwait concert which Carl Robert gave me before we left, and threaten to confiscate it. Clive says the problem is that they won't let in a video unless it's first seen by the censor, and that takes a fortnight. It looks as though I shall lose it before I've even seen it, but, after disappearing into an office with the officials, Clive emerges to say that he has agreed to take charge of it himself and ship it straight over to London in the earliest B.C. diplomatic bag.

We check in at the Sheraton Hotel, where we are introduced to a cool-eyed Dane called Steig Pederson, who is the Sales Manager. (Sheratons have no shortage of managers.) He takes me to a roof-top restaurant for a Press conference—Clive thinks he'd better come too 'to ward off any awkward questions about the Palestine problem'. Little chance of me wading in there! Nobody turns up for about 45 minutes, then I do a radio interview with a coal-eyed beauty from AM Radio and a newspaper piece with an intense Indian lady who hopes to 'get at the man behind the musician'—in ten minutes. It's taken most people sixty years, and they're still trying!

At 5 p.m., my afternoon nap is interrupted by a phone call from Mr Ahmed O. Ender, the hotel's Food and Beverage Manager, who wants to see me 'in five minutes' to discuss the arrangements. I call Sian's room and take her down with me, thinking that I might need some moral support. We're doing two shows here. On Friday, it's the official British Council concert, tomorrow is a sort of dinner dance for the hotel itself, to repay it for giving us accommodation. Naturally, Mr Ender is more interested in this Sheraton function, and gives us a detailed schedule that includes playing while the guests are eating. Sian quashes this in her best Joyce Grenfell voice, saying icily, 'I don't think the British Council is all that interested in providing music for eating.' In the end, it's agreed that we do two normal sets after the meal, with a long interval in the middle.

There's a reception at Clive Mogford's tonight, but we're not sure how substantial the food will be, so I have a precautionary snack in the Coffee Shop at six. It has a South Sea Island décor and is staffed by Pekingese-faced Filipino lovelies with their names on lapel tags. My waitress is called Germalina. At 7.30 a car collects us to take us to Clive's place. It's actually only just across the road from the hotel, but 'the road' is a busy four- or five-way inter-section like Brands Hatch, so it's safer to take a five-minute trip around the one-way system. If I were not in the habit of keeping this diary I would have to find a substitute to record and memorize the names of the British Council wives, which tend towards the unusual and exotic. In Doha the wife of a British Council head Donald Munro was called Ramseya, here Clive's Indian wife is Opeta (there's a useful mnemonic in the repertoire of black vaudeville singer Billy Banks who, with his Rhythmakers, recorded a song called 'Oh Peter' in 1932).

There are lots of VIPs at the party, including the British Ambassador. I am invited by the Pakistani Regional Manager of the Khaleed *Times* for lunch on Friday, an invitation which is extended recklessly to the whole band before the party's over. The purpose appears to be for us to lend a professional ear to his 12-year-old son playing the organ. He is, we are given to understand, a prodigy. One never knows how firm these party-time invitations are, but the R.M. is very insistent, giving me his card which reveals that his name is Arshad Sami Khan. No far-fetched mnemonic needed here—from now on he will be Sammy Cahn. He has a rival at the party in the form of a portly Sikh who edits the Gulf *Times*. He gets in on the act by marshalling a group of us, including Mr and Mrs Mogford and the Ambassador and his wife, for a photograph, the Khaleed *Times* having neglected to send a photographer along to the party. As we all beam into the camera, the be-turbaned editor cries, 'Now I have a scoop!' Well, yes, but a mild one.

Thursday, 14 January 1982, Abu Dhabi
We get free copies of the Gulf *Times* in the hotel. Mine, delivered to my room, reveals that the editor achieved more of a scoop than even he imagined. The faces are there, but all the names are either misspelt or transposed in the caption. 'Mr C. Magford' swops places with the British Ambassador, acquiring his wife in the process, while the face identified as the Ambassador's lady belongs in fact to someone who arrived in Abu Dhabi yesterday and just happened to get into the picture.

A note from Sian Griffiths has been pushed under my door while I slept to say that the lunch invitation on Friday is NOT for the whole band but for me alone. Sammy Cahn apparently rang early this morning to make this clear, having presumably been soundly ticked off by his wife for having spread the invitation to all and sundry in a burst of festive euphoria. It's becoming an awkward situation, as I don't fancy going off on my own for a whole afternoon.

They have a splendid pool at the Sheraton, where one can lie in the sun, eavesdrop on sundry business conversations involving billions of dollars, and hoist a pennant on a miniature flag-pole for the pool-side service, a luxury that brings out the Lord de Vere in Roy Williams, who is enjoying

'Ear-Bew-Dear-Beer'. From time to time an attendant comes round among the sun-beds with a message on a blackboard, calling a guest to the telephone. In mid-morning, I see my name on the board, summoning me to speak to a Miss Clare McFord. Who is this lady? I already have a date with someone called Angela Trew, who sounds like the skipper of an Angela Brazil hockey team but is in fact going to interview me for the local Capital Radio station. When I get to the phone I discover that it is Clive Mogford who wants to speak to me, to say that he too has been invited to Sammy Cahn's tomorrow but doesn't want to go. On the other hand, the Regional Manager of the Khaleed *Times* is someone to keep in with, is a good friend of the British Council's, etc . . . I decide there and then that it is up to me to do a Captain Oates. I will go on my own—but not for lunch. I will go for tea at 5 o'clock, with a pre-arranged get-out at 7 to prepare for the concert. So that's settled. As it is, I have to leave the pool at 3 o'clock today to go across to the radio station—in the same block as Clive's flat—to be interviewed. Angela Trew is well-briefed and asks good questions—which means plenty of stuff about the present and immediate past, not too much harping on the ancestors, Eton and the Guards. If there is anyone still around who doesn't know that I bought my first trumpet when playing truant from the Eton and Harrow match in 1936, he's unlikely to be listening to an English-speaking radio station in Abu Dhabi— he'll be too busy still fighting World War II.

Tonight is the hotel's informal 'do', with the audience at tables, a buffet supper half-way through, and dancing if they want to. Our band-room is a small, curtained-off cubby-hole behind the stage, at the opposite end of the ballroom from the one exit. At the finish, there is such a prolonged uproar of appreciation that the only way we can get out and up to bed is to strike up 'When the Saints Go Marching In', march through the cheering crowds, out of the far door and straight into the lift. In the interval, I met Harry Brown's sister who lives out here. He is a bit of a recluse now, they say, and when she comes to England and looks him up in Clapham, he won't answer the door. I offer to find out how he is, if I can.

Friday, 15 January 1982, Abu Dhabi
The Sheraton staff are all smiles this morning after the scenes last night, especially as it was their function. We are now people of some importance. As befits VIPs, we spend the day lounging arrogantly by the pool. It's just as well that the skies are still clear blue, as a member of the ruling family of the United Arab Emirates has died this morning, and the TV channels are full of wailing and rocking to and fro, and there's only a Tom Jones movie on 'in-house' TV.

At 5 p.m. I'm picked up by Sammy Cahn and taken to his house. Over tea and sweetmeats, I listen to his plump 12-year-old son play the organ. The story is that, while on foreign service in Portugal, Sammy senior bought the organ but couldn't get on with it himself. One day he came home unexpectedly and heard Sammy junior playing it, picking out tunes and harmonies with remarkable facility for a (then) eight-year-old. The family returned to Pakistan where the boy was taken up by a local music teacher, and soon had a regular spot on TV. But Papa was a supporter of Mr Bhutto and got thrown out, settling in Abu Dhabi. Fortunately for me, the boy is extremely good—his repertoire is cocktail bar music with no scope for originality but his harmonies and 'time' are perfect. There is talk of him going to America and, since he already has an American accent and a self-confident air, I am able to say with sincerity that he should do well there. I feel rather sorry for his younger brother, who has a bad stammer and is probably overshadowed. I get him to sing for me—he croaks out some very out-of-tune rock 'n' roll and grins broadly with satisfaction. If Sammy Cahn junior becomes famous, I shall claim that I discovered him.

Tonight it's the British Council concert at the Sheraton with its seated audience, a less frenzied affair than last night. A former Mick Mulligan band bass-player, Frank Thompson, comes into the little backstage alcove that serves as a bandroom with a couple of young friends. I think they helped themselves to some of our beer but I shall say nothing. The last time I saw Frank was in a restaurant near the BBC TV Theatre at Shepherd's Bush. He'd just returned from abroad and asked about all the old faces. When I told him that George Melly had just written a book (*Owning Up*) all about the Mulligan days, he turned to his wife and said, 'We must go out and get that tomorrow!' When I got home and looked him up in the book, I discovered that the nicest thing George says about him is that he had green teeth.

Tomorrow we drive across the desert to Dubai.

Saturday, 16 January 1982, Dubai
Picked up in a minibus at the Sheraton by one of the Jebel Ali Club people. The drive across the desert is monotonous, the miles of scrubby sand relieved only by endless hoardings advertising hi-fi and kitchen equipment, by the occasional camel and by the carcases of innumerable cars. Someone has told us that the deep Islamic conviction that Allah will ordain the future rules out the concept of long-term maintenance. It amounts to blasphemy to suggest that a driver must make provision for anything further than the immediate future. So when a car goes wrong, its owner drives it out into the desert, dumps it and hitches back to town to get a new one. We pass some pretty expensive wrecks, some with bonnets gaping as if they died gnashing their jaws in a desperate struggle.

Sunday, 17 January 1982, Dubai
Our visit to the Jebel Ali Club yesterday and today has been virtually a carbon copy of the 1979 trip, except that what was a chilly concert then is an absolutely freezing one tonight, with a consequently dampening effect on the audience. In the second half I encourage them to dance, to stop them lapsing into premature rigor mortis. One new feature this year is that I am given an Indian 'house boy' to dance attendance on me in my executive bungalow. He is a mature Indian gentleman with the unlikely name of Mr Nicholas, and he's there all the time, hovering expectantly. On Saturday lunchtime at the Club, I say to them, 'Thanks for the thought, but I don't know what to do with him.' They are astonished. 'Well . . . er . . . give him orders!' In the afternoon I dig out some laundry for him to do, and suggest he might iron my band jacket. On returning to the villa from the swimming pool, I find him standing in the living-room with a cylindrical sofa cushion on his left arm, over

which he has draped my jacket. Stroking away with the iron in his right hand, he looks like Yehudi Menuhin in lyrical action.

On Sunday morning, he reports for duty some time while I am still asleep. When I pad along to the kitchen at 8.30 for a drink of water, he is sitting there patiently, having waited for over an hour for me to wake up and start issuing orders. After he has provided some breakfast and, later, a mid-morning coffee, I defy the strict instructions of his employers and stand him down for the rest of the day. If an unscheduled half-day off is really going to undermine his discipline and threaten the whole system, then it's time they changed it.

Monday, 18 January 1982, Jeddah
Leave Jebel Ali for Dubai Airport at 6.30 a.m., to fly to Jeddah. A circuitous route this time, changing planes at Bahrain and stopping off at Dahran in Saudi Arabia to queue into, and then out of, immigration before re-embarking. On the last lap, berobed male Arab passengers keep disappearing into the toilets, to emerge later clad in gleaming white high-quality towelling, sans head-dress. These, it transpires, are pilgrims en route to Mecca and the posh towelling represents the humble sackcloth of tradition. Arriving at Jeddah at 12.45 local time, we are met by a tall, ginger-haired Maurice Denham lookalike, who sees us through customs with a quiet unflappability befitting a country in which the potential for diplomatic flaps must be limitless. The customs men buzz like bees around our instruments, taking all the instrument cases out of the flight box and starting to rip off the padded lining until a shriek from Sian deters them. At the immigration desk, Michael warns us not to say that we are here to play music, but simply to put 'Guests of the British Ambassador' as the purpose of our visit. They seem quite happy to accept that guests of the Ambassador customarily arrive with musical instruments, including a double bass and complete set of drums.

I am indeed a guest of the Ambassador, being put up at the Embassy throughout this trip. Over lunch, Sir James Craig is entertaining and fascinating on the subject of his recent tribulations. The 'Mrs Arnot' whom we met at Tim King's

125

party here in 1979 has since become a leading and universally-known figure in the Helen Smith Case, as has her husband who was even then languishing in jail for his involvement in the 'drinks party' from which the scandal arose. In addition to this, Sir James has had to weather the Death of a Princess Affair, the row over the British TV film which led to him being ordered out of the country for a while. He is interesting, too, about the complex facts behind Saudi Arabia's reputation for Islamic strictness. The Wahabi sect that rules Saudi is sterner even than Khomeini's Iranian Shi'ites, whom it regards as given to frivolity. The rigmarole at the immigration desk was due, it seems, to Wahabi law forbidding music, dancing or indeed the relishing of food over and above the call of sustenance. It occurs to me while he is telling us this that there is incongruity in the appearance of Jeddah itself—the run-in from the airport has blossomed, since our last trip, into a sky-scrapered, neon-lit, glass-clad imitation of, say, Zurich or Dusseldorf. The recollection of a smart new Habitat show-room near the city centre seems at first ill-matched to the talk of worldly austerity but, on reflection, shiny red plastic chairs that spill you on to the carpet if you recline too steeply are clearly designed to conform to Wahabi severity.

The whole lunchtime conversation throws light on the paradoxes and contradictions which one encounters in the official Arab attitudes. A story that is told round the table sums it up. On the quite recent State visit to Britain by the Saudi ruler and his government, they were entertained at a Lord Mayor's dinner at the Mansion House. The King and his Ministers and/or relatives (the two are often synonymous) sat together, with the Imam—religious adviser—on the King's right hand. At the end of this isolated row was a minister who found himself sitting next to an ample lady in a low-cut, off-the-shoulder dress. He sent a message along the line to the Imam asking for guidance. The reply was passed back: 'Speak with her, but do not look at her.' When the meal had been under way for some time, another message was passed along from the Imam: 'Contrary to my instructions, the Minister is looking at the lady.' Back went the message: 'Another question—how does the Imam know that I am looking at the lady unless he too is looking at her?'

At 4.30, a bespectacled young man called Chris Anander—a member of the concert committee that is putting on our shows—turns up to take me to look at the venues, both private affairs in schools, divorced from the British Council. The rest of the band are lodged in the vast, impersonal, Swiss-owned Nova Park Hotel, partly perhaps because one of the embassies now contributing to the concert committee is Swiss, and also for the good reason that the Sands Hotel, our home-from-home last time, is currently occupied by Idi Amin. There's a party this evening at the Swiss Ambassador's house, not, for a change, a stand-up buffet but a comparatively formal sit-down dinner at the start of which the Ambassador makes a formal speech of welcome. There is a lady there called Angela whose face I recognize but can't place. Aware that I must have met her somewhere, I screen her conversation carefully for clues, without success. After a while she waxes autobiographical and the penny drops—I have seen her on programmes at home such as 'Pebble Mill at One' and 'Good Afternoon', campaigning on behalf of female sufferers from cystitis. She has founded a self-help society and writes books about it. She is here for other reasons, I gather. I've no doubt the problem exists in Saudi Arabia as elsewhere, but I should imagine it's centuries away from a public airing.

Tuesday, 19 January 1982, Jeddah
Cup of tea brought in the morning by Ali, the North Yemenite 'house man'—no colonial talk of 'house boys' here. He is an imposing, totally silent matchstick figure in a gleaming white robe, a tiny knotted turban perched on a head like a shrivelled conker. You have to have an O-level in headgear to know exactly who you're dealing with over here. Given a square piece of cloth and the necessity of draping it over the head, an extraordinary range of styles and techniques has developed, each one imparting a vital piece of social information. The Kuwaitis are the flash boys, wearing their white tea-cloths with a certain panache and pulling the brow-piece forward into a frilly peak that takes some skill to achieve. On the Red Sea side they seem to favour a more martial style, with one drape of the square flung across the lower face like a

scarf and Clint Eastwood eyes glinting through the narrow gap that's left. Royalty seems to favour drapes that hang straight down like blinkers—with Freudian significance, perhaps. Presiding over subjects who range from cosmopolitan to tribal, it must be useful to see only what you want to see.

Breakfast at 9.30—His Excellency is long since up and away. Then it's out to the pool, a smallish rectangle reflecting splendidly the British way of life. No luxurious sun-beds or gaudy sun-shades, just a few old metal and plastic chairs, most of them three-legged or deficient in vital elements of the seat. The band come across from the Nova Park Hotel, the swimming pool there having been designed so that for most of the day, it lies in the shadow of the hotel tower block. We stick out the heat, the flies and the discomfort until lunchtime, when a huge dish of sandwiches is brought out, courtesy of the Ambassador.

The concert tonight is in a big gymnasium with acoustics that swallow up most of my announcements. Rather a disappointing affair after the euphoric open-air shows last time. After it we go to a party held by a couple in the British Embassy. At one point I am surrounded by a group of young people all eager to discover the rules of 'Mornington Crescent'. This enigmatic party game from the BBC radio quiz 'I'm Sorry, I Haven't a Clue', of which I am the hapless chairman, has exercised the minds of listeners over the eight years or so since we first started the show. On its first appearance, I introduced it as 'the children's' game which all of us have played in our time'. Thenceforward, we have not thought it necessary to explain the rules on which the team-members Tim Brook-Taylor, Willie Rushton, Barry Cryer and Graeme Garden base their carefully considered moves from one London Tube Station or street location to another towards the winning destination, Mornington Crescent. Consequently, we have all of us received a steady stream of letters saying, in effect, 'You may have played "Mornington Crescent" in your childhood, but some of us haven't . . .' and demanding an explanation. We think it's more fun to let people work it out for themselves, and it's gratifying to know that, in many house-holds, maps of the London streets and Underground system are unfolded and laid out whenever the programme comes on the air. It's giving away no secrets, I believe, to say that we once did a spoof version—a Pro-Celebrity game in which I pretended to introduce one of the distinguished knights of the British theatre. As a non-existent figure made his way to the stage, our well-briefed studio audience gave 'him' a rapturous welcome. Addressing an empty chair deferentially as 'sir', I explained that he would take his turn after Willie Rushton, fifth in the order of play. When it came to Willie's turn, he cried 'Mornington Crescent!' triumphantly, bringing the game to an end. With profuse apologies I sent our 'guest' back to his seat, omitting throughout to give the listening audience his name. A few weeks later, when the show was on the air, I received a letter at the BBC which, in apoplectic terms, accused me, the producer and the BBC of the grossest discourtesy to one of our most distinguished actors. The producer had one or two similar complaints, and I've no doubt some went straight to the Director General. It was intriguing to discover that all the writers identified the 'guest', who naturally made no utterance during the programme but seemingly accepted his humiliation with the greatest dignity, as Sir Alec Guinness!

At the party, I plead that the rules of the game are too complex to be explained at such a late hour, and eventually retire to bed leaving them none the wiser.

Wednesday, 20 January 1982, Jeddah
Visit to the souk in the morning—the concert committee has put a car at our disposal whose driver, they say, will act as our guide. He is a grumpy young man who clearly has other ideas. He drops us off at the car park and clears off, after arranging to pick us up two hours later. Arab self-consciousness about the not-so-distant primitive past has led to great chunks of the old souk having been demolished since our last trip, to be replaced by something more like a Western shopping centre. But fortunately, conservationists—mostly Western, I suspect— have got the message through that there is something to be said, on the commercial, touristic level, for retaining the picturesque section at the top with its photogenic old wooden buildings and colourful spice and food stalls, so the demolition has been stopped, at least for the time being. The best bargains

now, they say, are pirated cassettes. That, in effect, means *any* cassettes—classical, pop or jazz—since the ripping-off of Western recording companies is a major industry here and counterfeit cassettes, indistinguishable from the originals but copyright-free, are on sale for the equivalent of about 70p each. Ever since I've been on the receiving end of promotional records and cassettes at the BBC, I've got out of the habit of paying money for them, so I save my 70p's and buy yet another Bedouin head-dress instead—a red and white check this time, Saudi style.

Yesterday, Chris and Primrose Anander offered to take the birdwatching enthusiasts among us out to look at flamingo and black kites. The sewage outlet and the rubbish tip didn't sound quite so enticing as, say, Minsmere or the Ouse Washes back home, and they did ask rather anxiously if we are sensitive to smells. We accepted without reservation, and they pick us up after lunch. The first port of call is a bit strong, a huge, malodorous swamp steaming slightly under the afternoon sun, but offering in compensation a fine view of scores of pale-pink, Arabian-type flamingo, as well as more familiar sanderling, redshank, curlew, sand-piper and little plover in scurrying abundance. From the sewage outlet we drive further out to the rubbish tip—a spectacular journey, since the road eventually peters out into a sand-track, while remaining ostensibly a big dual carriageway. Apart from us, the traffic consists exclusively of lorries and juggernauts, most of which pound in both directions along the comparatively smooth central reservation, swerving like huge dodgem cars to avoid collision. This road out to the tip is lined by a veritable shanty-city of dumped containers, some of which have been adapted, with windows and doors cut out, for some kind of nomadic human occupation. Chris Anander points out that, with consumer goods entering in containers and oil going out in tankers, the importing companies from the West have a problem as to what to do with their 'empties', and despite fines and embargoes imposed by the Saudis, still find it cheaper to dump the containers and travel light on the return trip. So a conurbation roughly the size of Watford has grown up outside the city, expanding daily as the heavy transporters continue to bucket and career to and fro.

130

But the sights en route are nothing compared to the first view of the tip itself. I am prepared for a sort of glorified municipal dump, the usual conglomeration of household refuse, soggy cardboard boxes, indestructible plastic objects and broken bottles. What confronts us on arrival at the tip is a vast and picturesque lagoon, a vista of lakes, beaches and islands in handsome monochrome under the late afternoon sun. It's only when we get out and walk about, binoculars at the ready, that we find out that the beaches consist of a shingle of rusty soft-drink cans—millions and millions of them—and the islands are made up of the decomposing bodies of old cars and trucks. The place is alive with birds, not all easy to spot among the debris. Black kites are commonplace, and we are more excited spotting waders, varieties of heron, and black-winged stilts trailing their fragile legs behind them in flight like streamers. At one point, focusing on a pair of heron on a distant 'island', I spot a movement in a car wreck in the middle distance and discover a bird—shaped like a bittern but more probably a squacco heron—preening itself on the steering wheel. We could have stayed there for hours, but after a while a persistent itching around the ankles and moving up the trouser legs suggests that the lagoon's insect life is as interested in us as we are in the birds, and we beat a reluctant retreat. The journey back along the desert road is even hairier than the outward journey. Though there are two carriageways, the general rule seems to be that if the southbound road proves too deeply pot-holed, it's OK to veer across to the northbound lane and carry on against the tide. In a small saloon car, it must be like finding oneself in the path of stampeding elephants.

The evening concert, in a smaller, more intimate school hall, goes better than last night, and there's a bumper meal again at the Swiss Ambassador's, after which I talk several nice Americans into the ground.

Thursday, 21 January 1982, Sana'a
For once, not a crack-of-dawn start. In fact there is time for some mutual photography between myself and the Bangladeshi 'house man', Sayed, on the Embassy lawn after breakfast, by way of leave-taking. He snaps everyone who stays and must

have a rogue's gallery of top people. No 'to tip or not to tip' problems—a card on the bedside table 'suggests' the exact amount appropriate to each member of staff. Waiting for Michael 'Maurice Denham' Gathercole to pick me up, I browse among the Embassy bookshelves. The living-room is lined with erudite books on both Scotland and Arabia, the actual and spiritual homes of Sir James. In the hall, there's a small bookshelf full of 'naughty' novels—for the guests?

At the airport we check in the baggage, then sit down for buns and coffee in the small cafeteria. An official from Yemeni Airlines comes in, counts heads and says the Yemeni equivalent of 'OK, let's go!'—half-an-hour before the scheduled departure time. The unflappable Michael says, 'You're lucky—it could have been five hours the other way.'

We're met at Sana'a Airport by Ken Rasdall (see Kuwait, 1979), who has been doing for Sana'a what he did for Kuwait, that is, acting as administrative advisor in the teething stages of a new airport. We have told him in advance that we have a new drummer this time. When introduced to Sian in her travelling 'uniform' of open-neck shirt and jeans, he says, 'And this is the new man, eh?' Sian is the antithesis of 'butch', but the combination of jeans, height and shortish curly hair sometimes confuses. I don't know which makes her crosser—being addressed as 'Monsieur' or 'Sair' by hotel porters or persistently as 'Sean' ('Shawn') by male British Council colleagues. (She is 'Sharn'.) Incidentally, Arab porters really do say 'sair' for 'sir', as in old *Punch* cartoons.

Ken Rasdall looks at our massive flight box and the white double-bass coffin and warns us that this is not Kuwait and he can't promise to get us through the formalities so easily. A first look at the airport staff is unpromising, too—wearing small turbans, grey or brown calf-length skirts and huge curly daggers in the sporran position, they look like brigands and pirates out of *Sinbad the Sailor*. However, within a few minutes Ken returns and beckons us through the Customs gate without a case being opened.

My theory that Nature packages human beings in near-identical sets, is confirmed when we meet the British Council representative, Peter Clark. He is a dead ringer for my old friend Max Jones, but with hair. (Max, the doyen of British jazz critics for many years, suffered alopecia as a young man, and in jazz circles his beret and shaded glasses are more famous than Dizzy Gillespie's were in the early days of Bebop.) Peter even shares Max's conversational flow and vocal timbre. Uncanny.

One of the reception committee, a big, lumbering man called Bob, is delegated to drive two or three of us to the hotel in a rattling Land Rover. Just outside the airport he decides to take a short cut along a bit of one-way road. Round a bend he meets a shrieking convoy of police motor cycles escorting a black Mercedes. They part to avoid him but drive on. 'Whoops,' he says, 'that was the President.'

Sana'a is 9,000 feet above sea-level and the air is rarified. When we check in at the newly-built Sheraton Hotel, they warn us to take the lift at all times—walking upstairs can leave you gasping for oxygen. After an hour's rest, we're picked up to go to Peter's house for drinks. Several people turn up to collect us, all in rattling jeeps or Land Rovers. The reason for the rattling—and for the predilection for four-wheel-drive vehicles—becomes apparent as we career off along streets that seem to have been specially prepared as a vehicle assault course. Lumps and pot-holes abound, and from time to time the cars crash into shallow trenches that jar them from axle to roof. The safest way to travel is to hang on to something above your head and lift your bum off the seat, to avoid mayhem among the vertebrae.

Sana'a is a small city—its panorama can be taken in from one window of the Sheraton Hotel, which is on a hill above it. On the outskirts are rows of rickety stores—lock-ups really, whose iron garage doors are decorated with gaudy patterns in bright primary colours. Design and decoration are a feature of the place. Nearer the centre the city sprouts taller buildings whose brownish mud-colour is alleviated by elaborate patterns daubed round and between the windows. There's pattern and gaiety, too, in the women's attire. As in the other Arab countries, they are heavily shrouded from head to foot, but here it is layers of what look like gaudily-dyed tea and table cloths that preserve their modesty. The men in their skirts and daggers would be all right if it wasn't for the jackets—sad, Western affairs seemingly from an Oxfam consignment of old demob suits. The daggers, we are told, symbolize manhood and are proudly acquired by boys in their early teens on what I suppose would be the equivalent of their bar-mitzvah.

Peter Clark's house is tucked away in a narrow sidestreet. 'When in Rome . . .' is clearly the firm policy of Peter and his wife Theresa and they prefer to live in less well-appointed but more picturesque Arab style rather than on one of the modern, Western-style estates. We troop up narrow stone stairs and remove our shoes before going into the living-room. This is a long rectangle furnished almost exclusively at floor level, with cushions along three of the walls onto which we gratefully subside. Very comfortable and relaxing, except that the Clarks' baby son Gabriel, at the crawling stage, cruises round the room like Swee'pea in the Popeye strip, knocking over all the drinks. High up at one end of the room is a round stained-glass window—Peter explains that stone masonry and stained glass work are two North Yemen specialities, the skills exported all over the Arab world. Under the influence of Peter's hospitality, the Arabian ambiance and undulating Yemeni music on a cassette-player, life has suddenly become totally euphoric and unreal.

In this mood we go on to Ken Rasdall's house, as guests at his birthday party. He and his wife Anne also live in a traditional Yemeni house with barely-furnished, cell-like rooms which would seem chilly and uninviting but for the consistently warm climate that rules out the need for floor, wall and window coverings. The Rasdalls' friends swarm like gannets round a sensational assortment of curries, salads and sweets. I remember Ken's curries from our '79 Kuwait trip, but here he surpasses himself. A lady called Rosa dispenses mulled claret of her own making using, so far as I can tell, the concoction of red wine, brandy, Cuisenier, water, sugar, cinnamon and cloves which I splosh together for Christmas parties at home. I have always thought it a mild brew, but combined with the rarified air it has obviously acquired lethal powers, knocking out Mick Pyne, Theresa Clark and finally— and dramatically—Rosa herself, who actually hits the floor. A wonderful evening.

Back at the Sheraton, euphoria merges into nightmare as I try to watch *Saturday Night Fever* on a hotel room TV that's on the blink. The characters gargle like robots and are periodically suffused in blood-red blobs, making John Travolta look like a crazed mustang from some far-fetched horror movie. Sensing delirium on the way, I switch off and lapse into a dreamless sleep.

Friday, 22 January 1982, Sana'a
Am taken sightseeing in the morning by an American couple, John and Susan Giusti, with their two children. The expatriate community here is far smaller than that in the oil countries and seems to be limited to diplomats, cultural representatives and teachers. We go to the souk and are immediately immersed in Arabia—the real thing, as opposed to 'the Gulf' or 'the Middle East'. Overlooked by the tall, white-patterned buildings, the market stalls are crowded into a labyrinth of narrow streets. The whole scene is alive with every colour and shade in the spectrum, and the noise is indescribable. Yemeni Arabic is spoken, or rather shouted, in something between a bark and a quack, and the nearest thing I've ever heard to the sound of Sana'a in full cry is at Loch Leven in Kinrosshire when the greylag geese flock in from the pastures. Along one street, peering through an open door into semi-darkness, we discern the ghostly shapes of three camels circling in a stately minuet round a stone corn-grinder.

There are plenty of unusual things to buy. Unlike most of the Gulf cities, Sana'a actually has a long history, and the presence of a large Jewish population until quite recent times ensures a great variety of antiques. The Yemeni Jews were renowned silver-smiths, and the old silver jewellery—heavily embossed and encrusted bracelets and huge neck-pieces like mayoral chains of office, all with a deep, blue-grey, pewterish tint—are magnificent. I buy a thick bracelet bearing the authentic mark of a Jewish silver-smith and enough knobs, blobs and excrescences on it to fell an assailant with one blow. For myself, there are more articles of clothing to be bought for my Arab wardrobe—a terracotta square for the turban and a rather natty grey worsted skirt or *footah*. I have my eye on a dagger (*jambia*) but it will take some shopping around—there are piles of new ones with gleaming stainless steel blades and

135

pristine pigskin scabbards, but I want something more time-worn. I'm too old to go round looking like a novitiate! There's such a cheerful, anything-goes atmosphere in the souk that I am emboldened to put on the skirt and turban there and then. The store-holder volunteers to knot the turban for me in an authentic style, and seems unperturbed when I put the skirt on over my trousers. John Giusti tells me that there are several regional variations in the way the turban is tied—a fact that's confirmed when I walk off down the street and am confronted almost at once by a portly Yemenite who stops in front of me with arms outstretched in greeting and bellows the name of his village several times, pointing at my head-dress. All along the way my eccentric attire inspires smiles and salutations, a change from the Gulf atmosphere in which the wearing of Arab gear by Europeans invites often justified suspicion. At one stall, where I buy a selection of the women's patterned headscarves for Jill and Georgina back home, the stall-owner spots my camera and insists that I take a picture of himself, his brother, his cousin, two sons and a nephew with the entire Giusti family, all sprawling among the haberdashery in postures of camaraderie. Five minutes earlier, he and John had been slanging each other in a bout of heavy bargaining. The Yemeni attitude to cameras is the opposite of the discouragement we found in Jeddah. Here everybody wants to be photographed—small boys pose in front of one, grinning delightedly when they hear the click and undeterred by the fact that they will never see the results.

We talk of coming back here if possible this afternoon, but John gives us an odd look and says, 'If you're going to do any bargaining, leave it till the morning.' He then draws our attention to one or two passers-by who are carrying what look like switches of bay tree or green privet hedge. 'That stuff's called *gat*,' he says, 'they'll go home and chew the leaves after lunch, and when they come back, you'll get no sense out of them.' *Gat*, it seems, is a type of privet, the leaves of which have strong narcotic properties.

We've already seen one or two men sitting around with cheeks bulging but have attributed it to toothache. The technique, John says, is to stow the chewed leaves into one cheek until it will hold no more, then sit back and allow the juices to infiltrate the system, inducing euphoria and mild hallucination. A small branch well endowed with twigs and leaves can be bought in the souk for something like the equivalent of £12—at least £4 a cheekful, I would estimate, so oblivion is an expensive commodity here. It's also big business —the privately-owned (and quite legal) plantations are as heavily guarded as military installations, and penalties for breaking in are dire.

From the souk we go to an alfresco barbecue lunch at the home of John Bunney and his wife Pamela. He is Head of Chancery at the British Embassy and they have a smart, modern house with a small garden in which we sit in the scorching sun. The food is served by two startlingly beautiful Sudanese house-girls with faces as smooth as carved ebony and robes so gossamer-thin that the bright sunshine renders them virtually stark naked. Apart from that, the afternoon is relaxing and leisurely.

The concert tonight in the Sheraton Hotel has a small and select audience of about 150, including a party of twenty or so Yemeni students from the English school. It's true what they said about the air up here. From the start it's clear that we're going to have to adjust our breathing. A lungful lasts a fraction of the normal time, and when we come to the first slow number, with a lot of sustained notes, phrases can be heard petering out all over the shop. It's a good, lively concert, and afterwards we meet the audience in an adjacent bar. One of the young Yemeni students asks me reverentially how old I am. When I answer, 'Sixty', he looks duly awestruck and then says, 'Ah, well . . . you have the experience to make up for it.'

Saturday, 23 January 1982, Sana'a
A busy day ahead. Have prevailed upon a hirsute teacher called Dave to take myself and John Barnes to the souk at 9.30 this morning, so I can shop around for my *jambia*. I deeply suspect that J.B. is about to pull a stroke in our perennial battle of the dishdashers. He has had a look in his eye ever since Carl Robert gave me the grey and embroidered Sunday-best affair in Kuwait. Since then he's been determined to outdo me with something flashier.

Dave turns out to be a manic driver with a dent of locality where the bump should be. We career through the troughs and chasms of the main street at breakneck speed in his Land Rover, and I hang on to the back of the passenger seat so hard that it comes away in my hand. 'Never mind—just chuck it on the floor!' bellows Dave, jamming his foot down. At the souk we dash off in different directions in search of our respective quarry. In an antique shop I find just what I want—a *jambia* with a chipped, tarnished but razor-sharp blade, housed in a scabbard of weather-beaten leather with a mass of metal decoration. I don't know how old or authentic it is—perhaps it's a new one that's been cunningly 'distressed'—but, when the ornate woven belt has been let out to encompass my thick European waistline, it suits me fine. At the appointed meeting place J.B. turns up, jutting gleefully, with a loose parcel under his arm. As I suspected, he has trumped my Kuwait acquisition with a silky robe in black and white stripes.

When we get back to the vehicle it has a flat tyre. Such is the general air of goodwill that we hesitate to suspect foul play, but the gash which we find in the rear off-side wheel could conceivably have been made by a curly, sharp instrument. Dave changes the wheel before a huge gallery of passers-by. He's the sort of stocky, energetic character who flings himself somewhat erratically into every activity, and from the excited cackling and mirthful exposure of devastated gums among the male audience, you'd think he was performing one of Harry Tate's time-honoured motoring routines.

With the new wheel fixed, we rush back to the Sheraton just in time to perform a midday concert for schoolchildren. There are two hundred of them of all ages and nationalities with one language—twangy American—in common. Once again it's a lot of fun, and they blow some fine raspberries during the brass instrument demonstration. Immediately afterwards, a party of us is whisked off for lunch at Peter Clark's house. Theresa has done a marvellous meal in local style, with plenty of yoghurt and lentil dishes to satisfy Bruce's vegetarian requirements. We eat in the stone-walled kitchen, alongside a traditional Yemeni stove that looks like an Aga cooker roughly sculpted in mud. Then it's shoeless into the living-room to relax, listening to tapes of local musicians.

I ask Peter if he can prepare some cassettes of the music for me to take home and study at greater leisure. The problem with all Arab music is that it seems to have no time limit. To our uninstructed ears the voices seem to meander interminably among the tones and quarter tones without any noticeable highspots or climaxes to grab the attention. Like Kuwaiti music, the Yemeni songs have a strong rhythmic basis, but without drum support. The lute player (or players) strum out a frenetic accompaniment in unison with the voice, from which familiar rhythms—the habanera and beguine of Latin America, for instance—can be picked out. But the overall impression is closer to Indian music, with the words clearly playing an important part which we miss.

While we sit, Baby Gabriel is on the move again, cruising round the room as if by high speed clockwork. On one circuit he stops and crouches over my stockinged foot with his back to me. 'He's taking a great interest in your feet,' someone says jokingly, at which point I am racked with a sudden piercing pain in the big toe. I should have remembered that babies investigate the world with the mouth before hands and fingers—he's taken enough of my big toe into his mouth to give me a nasty nip in the sensitive area at the bottom of the nail. Luckily he doesn't care too much for the taste of my sock and lets go quite soon, leaving me with a sore toe and a tricky problem of etiquette. Does one ask a hostess for antiseptic when you've been bitten by her baby? You can't be too careful in this climate but one doesn't want to offend. I decide that Gabriel is more at risk from my sock, so keep quiet. If there isn't an Ogden Nash poem about catching rabies from babies, there should be.

Later in the afternoon, we go in a short convoy of rattlers to a nearby beauty spot—Wadi Dahr, a vast fertile valley overlooked by rocky hills from which the view extends to a hazy infinity. Our convoy drives to a promontory over which ravens soar—not the rare one or two which the eager birdwatcher might spot on Snowdon, but a dozen or more in one group. Down in the bed of the Wadi there's a small village dominated by a magnificent-looking square building, reddish-brown this time but with the familiar white patterns. It's mooted that we might go on down for a closer look, but Bruce

Turner's bad back has been fragmented by the trip to the summit over rocks and boulders, so we split up, some going back to the hotel, others putting their lives in the hands of Daredevil Dave the Demon Driver who has volunteered to take us on.

It's worth the risk. En route we pass a large fertile plantation, surrounded by fences and look-out towers like a wartime Stalag. '*Gat*,' says Dave. 'That lot's worth millions at twelve quid a branch, so it would be worth a break-in.' Funny business—the economics are a bit puzzling to me. If the entire male population uses it and it's both legal and profuse, why is it so expensive? Dave explains that Wadi Dahr is one of only two fertile valleys that serve Sana'a and surrounding districts, so there is a rarity value. Apparently the leaves have an extremely unpleasant bitter taste and, for full effect, must be stowed in the cheek for a long time. There must be easier ways of getting brainless.

From ground level, the Imam's palace—the huge building we spotted from above—is even more staggering. It climbs in steps to the summit of a huge red rock so that, from the front, it seems to grow out of it. With ravens and the ubiquitous black kites circling round it against a brilliant blue sky, it cries out for acknowledgement as a wonder of the world. On the way back, Dave takes an unscheduled right fork on impulse and we find ourselves lurching up a track just wide enough to accommodate one skinny goat. It's not until our way is barred by a boulder the size of a garden shed that he says 'I think I've taken a wrong turning.'

At the concert tonight, Peter Clark says it would be a good idea if I were to wear my Yemeni outfit, dagger and all, on stage. He says it will go down well, especially with the indigenous population. John Barnes has a head-dress, so after a bit of 'If you will, I will', we agree to dress up for the second half. Peter's Yemenite assistant ties the turbans for us authentically, and I don the skirt and dagger. J.B. goes on first to test the water and receives an acclaim just short of a standing ovation, so I emerge with confidence. Pavlova stepping on stage for her farewell performance could hardly have been more rapturously received. As I bow low in acknowledgement, the dagger digs deep into my crutch, bringing me effectively down to earth. The audience remains euphoric to the end, but I don't think I shall adopt it as a band uniform. The skirt is very comfortable and loose, but with bare legs and sandals below I am very conscious of my size thirteen feet. Unshrouded by sagging trouser hem they feel like skis. Altogether, the concert has a lovely atmosphere—the stage is adorned with pictures and poems done by the schoolchildren this afternoon, giving their impressions of our noonday concert. Afterwards, going into the men's loo still in my rig-out, I am ecstatically embraced and kissed by a gnarled Yemenite with decimated teeth and five days' growth of beard. When I relate this in the band-room, Peter Clark says enigmatically, 'Hmm—that can be interpreted in several ways.' I hurriedly change back into my trousers.

Sunday, 24 January 1982, Sana'a
Another early start. Call at 6 a.m. for a pick up at 7 o'clock. The rather ethereal sense of fantasy that our Sana'a sojourn has engendered is capped by my hotel bill, made out by the Filipino cashier and enchantingly headed 'Mr Little Son'. Ken Rasdall sees us off at the airport where, once again the flight captain decides to take off as soon as he has mustered a quorum of passengers.

We're met at Cairo Airport by British Council representative Peter Thompson, aquiline and bearded. 'A typical trad jazz face,' someone remarks, to discover minutes later that he used to play piano in the Leeds University Jazz Band. He tells me that he has a tape somewhere of the band performing with its resident singer, Barry Cryer. I must have a copy—it will enhance my authority as chairman of 'I'm Sorry, I Haven't a Clue' to have such a skeleton from Barry's past in hand.

Unfortunately, Peter initially blots his copy book on the administrative side by collecting us with a minibus that's far too small to take us and all the instruments, and compounds the offence by insisting that the double bass coffin *will* go in if loaded sideways or upside down or whatever. So we sit in the hot and dusty street outside the airport for forty-five minutes until, after a lot of abortive heaving and sweating, the point is conceded and alternative transport is hired for the heavy

142

instruments. During this trip I've been reading Jonathan Raban's book *Arabia Through the Looking-Glass*—an invaluable travelogue through the Arab mind for anyone going to the Middle East. I've skipped forward to the point where he makes the same jump from Sana'a to Cairo and am surprised to find that he found the former totally depressing and disorientating and was mightily relieved to reach the reassuring cosmopolitan hubbub of Cairo. Our reaction has been exactly the opposite —Sana'a was a dream (enhanced, I have to admit, by the existence of the modern Sheraton Hotel, which wasn't available when Raban was there), and Cairo at first sight threatens to be a nightmare. For one thing, the rich blue sky of North Yemen has been replaced by a jaundiced grey pall, humid and bilious. And in place of the cheery but detached independence of the mountain people, Cairo seems shrouded in a kind of seedy and grasping cynicism. Even the international banks in the airport tout for business, their clerks calling and beckoning from the exchange booths like the ladies in Hamburg's Herbertstrasse. 'Hold on to your wallets and don't take your eye off the baggage for a moment,' is Peter Thompson's advice as we wait for our transport.

We're checked in at Shepheard's Hotel. All musicians are romantics, and the very name on the band itinerary has aroused expectations of an evocative throw-back to colonial splendour. In fact, though the hotel still boasts, via a large plaque in the foyer, about its historic associations, it is not even on the same site as the old Shepheard's, which was destroyed by fire some years ago. The new Shepheard's is certainly an impressive pile with huge public rooms, a vast foyer and spacious corridors. But such vestige as there is of colonial authority and high-handedness is now wielded by the staff. It is of some importance to us, nursing our expenses, to know what the particular rate is for our hotel rooms. Peter tells us one thing, the heavy mob masquerading as reception clerks behind the desk tell us another. The statistics are complicated by the fact that rooms overlooking the Nile are more expensive than those at the back. We've already seen the Nile which, on this grey day, is the colour of cabbage soup, so there is no rush to go for the scenic rooms. It seems to me that every time I go to ask about our alleged 'special rate' at the desk, the deal gets slightly worse, so I give up. The hotel staff are all dressed for a provincial production of Aladdin, and they hover like vultures. 'Tips with everything' is clearly the motto here.

As it's early afternoon by the time we're finally checked in, we have a late lunch in a ship's ballroom of a restaurant upstairs with no less than six truants from the chorus of Forty Thieves in attendance. Everywhere porters sit at strategic points in the corridors, preventing one from carrying so much as a paper bag to or from the lift without having it grabbed and subsequently held to ransom.

Cairo

Half-way through the first day in Cairo my diary suddenly peters out, partly because of an itinerary over the following two days that barely gave us time to eat and sleep, let alone scribble a journal, but also perhaps due to my feeling that the best of this particular tour was over. I recall, in the evening of the first day, going for a casual walk through the city with some of the others and being assailed on all sides by shopkeepers importuning for business. One of them actually seized Mick Pyne's arm and hauled him into a shop to sample perfume. The routine is always the same: 'You American? . . . German? . . . Engleesh? Ah, I am in England two weeks ago . . . Piccadilly Circus . . . Lycester Square . . . Hyde Park . . . you see, I know them, eh?' Had we confessed to being American or German, the guide-book list of locations would have been just as pat. We were told later that the answer to give is 'Russki', at which they immediately abandon their efforts, the Russians having no reputations as big spenders. After a few blocks our nerves began to fray—it had been a long day—and one or two worthy and enterprising traders were told, in vain, to piss off! My jaundiced view of Cairo at first sight was not ameliorated when I decided to make a late night phone call home (it has to be late because evening is the best time to catch the family in, and we are four hours ahead in Egypt), and discovered that the only available outside line was away across the river at the President Hotel. I had to take a cab—Peter said, apropos the fare, 'He'll ask for two Egyptian pounds—give him one.' The trip took fifteen minutes, and I had to wait a further hour in the President Hotel foyer, queueing for the one phone that linked us with civilization as we know it. An Italian lady ahead of me spoke in stentorian tones for twenty minutes, apparently arranging her divorce with an errant husband in Rome. On both outward and return journeys the cabbies asked for two pounds and I gave them two. What the hell—there are times when one's not in the mood to play silly games. I prefer our straightforward English way—if a cabby says the fare is one pound, we give him two.

On Monday, 25 January we left early for Alexandria, where the first concert took place. There are two routes, one across the desert and the other longer one along the Nile. We decided to go for the quicker route, which would take us past the Sphinx and the Pyramids at Gysa for a quick glimpse, but as we approached it we became bogged down in an impenetrable traffic jam, through which the message came that the road was closed. So we trundled for something like five hours through one village after another, stopping for food in a sort of amusement park en route. The young man serving us took my money at the end, pleading that he had run out of change and would have to give me English money. When I checked it after we had set off again, most of it turned out to be Maltese. En route we passed houses with camel and donkey fodder stacked on the flat roofs, combining the functions of hay-stack and insulation. I have no recollection of the concert so it must have been uneventful. The hotel had a nice view encompassing a sandy bay above which one of the late and unlamented King Farouk's palaces nestled in the trees.

Next day we returned to Cairo by the desert road, stopping off near the end to take photographs of the Pyramids. The place swarms with touts with camels in tow, clamouring for a modelling fee. You have to pick your camera angle to get that impression of splendid desert isolation so familiar from the travel magazines. Point the wrong way and you'll catch buildings on the skyline or a string of coaches in the car park. Even with these signs of modern intrusion the Pyramids retain that massive aloofness of antiquity. Writers sometimes refer to great monuments 'looking down' on the tiny, temporal beings below, but it's worse than that. They don't look at you at all, but stare out over your head like venerable lions at the zoo, leaving you feeling totally irrelevant and rather silly.

The Sphinx may well have imparted the same feeling, but we only passed it on the road, Peter Thompson having warned us that we would only be swamped with touts if we alighted. From this viewpoint it was disappointing—smaller than we had expected and much closer to the main road and surrounding buildings. The one blurred photo that I managed to get from the bus shows a clutter of modern masonry in the foreground. We didn't really give it a chance to impress, because by this time we were in a hurry to get into Cairo and make use of the late afternoon for hurried sightseeing. The choice available in the time was either a quick visit to the Museum or a dash to the bazaar. Predictably, I suppose, John Barnes and I chose the latter, being escorted by a man from the British Embassy who knew the best shops to visit. It was a sight to see—a maze of little streets and alleys lined by one Aladdin's cave after another of more exotic, sophisticated and expensive treasures than in any of the Gulf souks. A sort of labyrinthine Bond Street in which we bought some silver bits and pieces to take home, and some more robes. They stopped being dishdashers when we crossed from the Gulf to the Red Sea, becoming 'thobes' in Saudi Arabia and 'jellabas' here. It'll be all one when we get home. After the '79 tour I sent one of them to the laundry in Barnet, writing 'dishdasher' on the list. It came back with the word crossed out and 'night-dress' substituted.

At one point, back in the hotel, I was staring out of my bedroom window over the Nile, thinking that I was beginning to enjoy Cairo now that it was almost time to go home, when I turned to see a sort of Grand Vizier standing in the room. His turban and robes were a rich damson colour and I can't be sure, but I think his shoes curled up at the toe. With long drooping nose and wisp of grey beard he might have looked impressive, but it was the wheedling look that gave away his purpose. 'You are leaving tomorrow, sair,' he said. I nodded. 'I shall not be here when you go.' 'Oh,' I said, 'I'm sorry about that,' and turned back to the Nile. He was obviously some kind of head porter or commissionaire, but having for two days tipped somebody whenever I so much as walked down the corridor, I didn't see why I should now reward a total stranger. After what seemed like five minutes I turned back into the room, to find him still there, a silent and immobile presence. I am normally a push-over for buying a quiet life with largesse, but this time irritation at the sheer blatancy of the demand took precedence. I busied myself pointedly with sorting postcards and folding clothes while he continued to stand there. At long last he gave a theatrical shrug and stalked off with that measured and wary gait with which cats extricate themselves from a confrontation. I half expected him to point at me from the door with forked lightning darting from his fingertips to turn me into a toad, but he went ambling off leaving me feeling pleased with—and surprised at—myself.

By the time we've done a good concert and enjoyed another hospitable reception afterwards, I am convinced that I could grow to love Cairo. We've had a good time with Peter Thompson, who retains a musician's outlook from his semi-pro days and has looked after us well. That's one thing about all this travel—you pick up some good mates along the way. Home tomorrow. Three-and-a-half weeks is certainly the longest I've ever been away at one stretch. It was to have been five weeks, but we've postponed the last lap in March. It's just as well that indifferent weather and a heavy schedule has kept us away from the swimming pools for three or four days. Some of the edge has been taken off the obscene sun-tans which we will bring back to families who have just endured the worst January since 1947! No wonder we're loaded with gold and silver and all the treasures of the Orient.

Monday, 8 March 1982, Beirut

Up at 5.45 a.m. to get to Heathrow for the 9.35 flight to Beirut on Middle East Airlines. It seems an early call, but there's the car to park in the long-term car park, the bass coffin and flight box to check in again and, with luck, time for a spot of breakfast before the flight's called. Sian Griffiths is with us as before.

All goes smoothly, and we have an uneventful flight to Beirut where, as always, there's a British Council man to welcome us. This time it's a small gingery Scotsman with a pepper-and-salt beard who introduces himself as Farquar Grant. We start addressing him as 'Fark-war' but he corrects us, saying that the correct Scottish pronunciation is 'Farker'. Not the sort of name you can comfortably shout across a crowded room. (It reminds me of a colleague in the wartime army whose name was—and I hope still is—Johnny Bastard. The Grenadier Guardsmen, whose barrack-room conversation was strung together by four-letter words, came over coy when called upon to address him, altering the name to 'Mr B'stard' with heavy emphasis on the second syllable. He would have none of it, shouting 'Bastard, Bastard!' to their intense embarrassment.)

The Beirut Airport car-park looks like a wrecked car dump. Headlamp sockets gape blindly, bumpers sag drunkenly, doors droop from their hinges. The British Council vehicles—Farquar's car and an open lorry driven by an Anwar Sadat lookalike—seem in relatively good nick, and we drive off into

149

the capital, passing check-points manned by raffish-looking soldiers en route. They are Syrian troops—'an invited occupation' is how Farquar's assistant Marych puts it—and they look pretty ferocious in their brigands' attire.

We are staying at the Mayflower Hotel, not far from the American University in West Beirut. It looks homely and familiar, wouldn't be out of place in Guildford High Street—the bar even has a pub sign, 'The Duke of Wellington', over its street entrance. As soon as we check in, we are invited by the manager to go straight into the bar for a welcoming drink on the house. Sitting there, I ask Farquar just what the political situation is at the moment. He draws sharply on the ubiquitous fag and indicates with a sidelong look that it's not the sort of thing you discuss in a crowded bar. But he does inform us that we'll probably hear plenty of gunfire during the night, but not to worry. Bullet holes in the big mirror behind the Duke of Wellington's counter suggest that the gunfire may not be all that distant. We are, after all, in the Hamra district, where several bombs have gone off recently. But amidst the noisy chatter of an English-looking pub, there's little feeling of apprehension.

Later in the evening, we all walk for ten minutes down to a restaurant called El Pacha, recommended by Farquar and Marych as accessible, cheap, and of reasonable standard. It's just the sort of place in which musicians feel at home—a glorified students' 'caff' buzzing with life where one can shout and laugh and swap noisy reminiscences without inhibition. The food's good, too—kebabs with assorted dips of houmous, aubergine purée etc., everything stiff with garlic. Early bed and a good sleep, despite some desultory gunfire in the distance.

Tuesday, 9 March 1982, Beirut
After breakfast in the basement restaurant (nobody but us there), we are taken down to the American University to set up for tonight's concert. An eager young Lebanese called John is in charge of the PA. Initially, he has the sound jacked up so high that our opening must have been heard in the foothills of the Shouf mountains forty miles away. I don't want to upset him—as a Lebanese he has enough problems. So with infinite

patience I get the volume gradually reduced until we have all we need in the small hall—just a touch of amplification on bass and piano. It's a familiar problem. Ever since the invention of the electric guitar, which is no more than a concoction of wood and curtain wires until it's plugged into the mains, the electrical engineers who used just to provide microphones and speakers have acquired delusions of grandeur. They call themselves 'sound mixers', with the implication that musicians and bands are simply there to provide the raw materials for their creative talents. They sit behind the huge consoles at the back of the auditorium, hairy, skinny young men wearing jeans like tourniquets and huge headphones, twiddling with knobs and fiddling with faders so that the soft bits are loud and the loud bits are deafening. In the Alex Welsh band, from which both John Barnes and Roy Williams came to me, they called them 'Marconis'. In his customary forthright manner Roy will say to me on stage, 'We've got a fucking Marconi at work here—I've told him, "For Christ's sake, just set the bloody mikes and piss off to the pub!"' Unfortunately, Marconis don't set up thousands of pounds' worth of equipment just to piss off to the pub, so it's a running battle. Lebanese John doesn't look too happy by the time we've got everything down to something like a natural sound. Even then, I'm none too confident—especially when, on leaving the hall, we pass an incoming posse of students carrying even more amplification equipment.

Out and about after lunch, we find the main Hamra shopping street remarkably chirpy, though pock-marked with shell and bullet holes. It has had no time to recover from the first devastating civil war in the mid-Seventies, but it wasn't entirely smashed up and retains the air of a sort of beat-up Oxford Street. In most areas prices are ridiculously low—John Barnes buys a pair of smart leather shoes from a street vendor for about £10, and cigarettes are the equivalent of £2 for a pack of two hundred. After a brief look round I retire for an afternoon nap—not easy, as my hotel room seems to syphon in an incredible racket from hooting and lurching traffic, a nearby school playground and a garrulous caged bird on one of the tenement balconies which I overlook.

We're picked up at 5.15 for the concert—an early affair

151

starting at 6 o'clock since people don't like to be wandering about late. A grey-haired, lugubrious but distinguished-looking gentleman called Mr Nebeel Ashcar is Beirut's leading jazz authority and critic—it's somehow reassuring to discover that even embattled Beirut resembles every city and town in the jazz-speaking world in having a doyen among jazz buffs! Nebeel is helping the British Council in the presentation here, and he was hovering about at this morning's rehearsal. This evening, as soon as I arrive, he comes across to urge me to dispense with all amplification—he clearly has as little confidence in John the Marconi as I have. And how right he is! The students whom we saw arriving with additional sound equipment this morning have since erected it, and all our carefully acquired sound balance turns out to have been scrambled, apparently to suit the needs of a team from the University whom I have given permission to film the concert for their archives. The first half is an acoustic disaster—the ensemble sounds run into each other in a muddy soup like drenched watercolours, solos come and go in volume without rhyme or reason, and from time to time the whole band is swamped in gargantuan booming from the double bass. In the front row, Nebeel Ashcar's face elongates, registering alarm and despondency. At half-time I stage a temperament, diplomacy having failed. By striding rapidly up and down the band-room with arms flailing, I persuade John that I am serious in my wish to have all microphones and speakers swept away. As a result the second half is perfect, Nebeel perks up and the international—predominantly student—audience erupts, keeping us at it until around 8.45. Afterwards, backstage, Nebeel introduces me to his son Anwar (Anwar Ashcar? It sounds like a long-drawn-out sneeze), who has a radio show and interviews me on tape. Then we're driven off to a reception, where a largely expatriate gathering makes a fuss of us and gives useful information as to what to buy, where to eat and so on.

Wednesday, 10 March 1982, Beirut
At about 8.30 this morning, there's a knock on my door. I call out cheerily, 'Shan't be long!' assuming that it's a chambermaid after the bed linen, but a muffled voice says, 'I have a gift from

152

the Manager'. I open the door to find a maid bearing flowers and a box of chocolate truffles. Nice—but what for? After breakfast, I go to the reception desk to thank the Manager, who tells me that the presentation was from Mr Mounir Sama'a, the owner of the hotel, who would like to see me in his office. There I find a small, dapper, middle-aged man who sits me down and makes an emotionally-charged and rather moving speech, thanking me for last night's concert and trying to express what it meant to him and his fellow-citizens. 'Like all our country I am in a hell of a mess psychologically,' he explains, 'and for two hours last night we are completely transported away from all our troubles.' He comes near to tears when he talks about Beirut's glittering past as the Paris of the Arab world. 'You wouldn't believe how beautiful our city was, and now look at it—all broken.' As a further practical gesture of appreciation, he rings through to reception and has my room changed, moving me to what turns out to be a sort of bridal suite in front of the hotel, away from the romping schoolchildren and that damn bird. And he invites all the band to have champagne with him later in the day. I feel great sadness for him and his compatriots, without being any the wiser as to the reasons why they are tearing each other and their prized city to bits. It's very similar to the surface situation in Northern Ireland, where everyone you speak to appears to be a neutral victim of the troubles and you get no hint of the allegiances that must lurk underneath.

Out shopping with John Barnes this afternoon, I buy a book called *Crossroads to Civil War* in a newsagent's, and resolve to do some homework. A glance through the photographs alone suggests that I'm in for a tough time—names like Iskandar Ghanim, Musa al-Sadr, Taqui al-Din al-Sulh and Ghassan al-Tuwayni don't lodge easily in a Westerner's memory, and it's easy to get lost among the Shihàbs, Salams and Shamuns at the top of the ruling tree. The Palestinian movement is awash with acronyms, too—a chart at the end of the book guides one, mind reeling, through the PLO, PLA, PNC, PSF, PNF, PFLP and PDFLP, each of which represents some subtle difference in outlook or policy. It'll be like unravelling Christmas tree lights with the hope that they'll illuminate at the end.

Tonight's concert, again at the American University, is a

success from start to finish, with the amplifiers and their problems banished. The students who have been video-ing the shows come backstage afterwards to film some interviews. One by one, we spout into camera our individual responses to the question, 'What does jazz mean to you?' It's the sort of question that invites drivel, and we duly oblige. I trot out the line about jazz being the only music ever to appeal to heart, head and feet simultaneously. Bruce, whose natural instinct must have been to say, 'Don't know, reelly' (his standard cop-out line), delivers a dusty homily on improvisation and Dave, overcome by post-concert euphoria, Lebanese wine and the high degree of pulchritude among the girl students, waxes positively lyrical. 'Jazz is my living . . . my life . . . my love,' he intones with deep sincerity, invoking a maudlin chorus of 'Yeah, Dave, that's beautiful . . .' in the background.

Thursday, 11 March 1982, Beirut

We have a concert tonight at Brummana, a village up in the mountains about twelve miles from Beirut. Farquar decides to send us up there in two taxis, with the gear following on a truck. No doubt he has his reasons, but it seems a precarious way to travel. All along the coast road out of the city there are check-points manned by ferocious-looking young men in a variety of scruffy uniforms. From my book on the civil war I have learnt enough to know that these are not only Syrian troops but Palestinian Army units and, further along, militia-men from other factions through whose territory we have to pass.

There's a hairy moment en route. We're driving along a cliff road looking straight out over the sea, with Roy Williams, Dave Green and Mike Paxton in the leading cab when, suddenly, those of us following see a soldier leap out into the road and take aim at their rear window with an automatic rifle. Our driver hoots frantically and they pull up, to be surrounded by shouting soldiers. We stop in front to investigate. What has happened is that, in answer to a query about his camera by Mike Paxton, Roy has put it to his eye to demonstrate just as the cab drove past an army post. He was simply pointing the camera out to sea without any thought of taking a picture, but the soldiers thought otherwise. At first they make as if to confiscate the whole camera, but after intercession by the two cab drivers—no doubt on the lines that we are mad but harmless Englishmen—they content themselves with ripping out the film. Unfortunately, it was near the end of the reel and contained all his shots from January's tour as well, but Roy is nothing if not philosophical, especially in the knowledge that, not two minutes earlier, a wild-eyed sentry has been taking careful aim at the back of his head.

We all hide our cameras under the seats for the rest of the trip, especially as we drive down into the heavily-devastated area on the boundary of West and East Beirut. Here we come into contact with recent history as seen on the TV newsreels at home. There are the gutted ruins of the Holiday Inn Hotel in which British tourists and newsmen were holed up for days in the first outbreak of civil war in '76. Other erstwhile luxury hotels with familiar names—the Phoenician, the St George—loom hollow and eyeless above foothills of rubble. On top of one mound of stone and brick, heavily-armed soldiers watching the road below lounge arrogantly on sofas and armchairs looted from abandoned apartments. We have plenty of opportunity to take all this in since there's a sluggish queue through the many check-points. It's a relief when the driver says, 'OK—finish!' and we speed towards open country.

At Brummana, we go straight to the Tivoli Cinema where we are to play tonight. By Odeon standards it's modest—no need for microphones in the smallish rectangular basement. While we're setting up and hanging about down there, we're introduced to an imposing man of Orson Wellesian girth with the face of an amiable toad—he's Mr Albert Rizk, the owner of the cinema and of a restaurant upstairs, to which he invites us all to a meal as soon as we're ready. Here, in a bright, vine-festooned dining-room with a view across to the mountains, we have a chance to take in the much-vaunted beauty of Lebanon. With snow-capped mountains in the distance, cattle grazing on the nearby slopes and firs, cypresses and stone pines softening the rocky outlines, the panorama combines the best of Switzerland and Italy. We're in the wrong place for the famous cedars of Lebanon, but this ambiance will do for the time being.

155

At Albert's table we gorge ourselves with dish upon dish of varied dips and stuffed leaves and meatballs. When someone rashly likens it to Greek food, Albert is incensed, and in a magnificently expensive voice like a gravel-toned Levantine Sydney Greenstreet, proclaims that 'Greek food is a travesty of Turkish food, and both are travesties of Lebanese food!' It's true that the selection here puts all previous Greek, Turkish and Cypriot experiences in the shade. When the dishes have all been replenished more than once, we begin to plead that we are full. 'Full?' cries Albert, appalled, 'but we have only just begun!' This feast, apparently, was merely the hors d'oeuvres —a procession of even larger dishes arrives at the table, mostly based on lumps of deliciously-marinated lamb, to be followed by a cream and syrup sweet which sends Bruce Turner into ecstasies. As we walk stiffly out of the restaurant at the end, vowing that this will be our last meal for forty-eight hours, Albert calls after us:

'Of course, you will be my guests at dinner after the concert tonight!'

We're staying at the Al Bustan Hotel in Beit Mery, a little village further up the hills. It's a huge pink and white building with an uninterrupted view down to Beirut and the sea beyond from which, they say, the spectacle of the city under bombardment during the hostilities was spectacular. Indeed, we are warned that if civil war should break out again, as it well may at any time, the valley below the hotel will represent, as before, the 'front line' between the major factions and we may expect the ground floor of the Al Bustan to be taken over by artillery. Incidentally, when we told the English people connected with the concert here about Roy's narrow shave en route, they were not in the least amused. Driving inadvertently past checkpoints without stopping when ordered is, they say, the commonest cause of death or casualty among expatriates. Most of the soldiers are trigger-happy kids and they don't waste time shooting at your tyres.

After a brief nap, it's back to the Tivoli for tonight's concert. Still groaning from the extended lunch, we're not exactly straining at the leash, but we find a wonderful atmosphere in the cinema, with a large, cheerfully noisy and predominantly young audience giving us a fine reception. We

156

can't be sure whether it's for our music or simply for our presence there. In the interval and afterwards, we encounter again the question with which we've become familiar on trips to Northern Ireland. 'Why have you come here?' they ask in genuine wonderment that anyone from a relatively safe and orderly part of the world would be so reckless. It's a hard one to answer without sounding condescending—in Belfast once, a somewhat abrasive interviewer interrupted my vague answer with: 'Are you doing us a favour, then?' at which I was stung to reply: "Not on your life—I'm getting a very good fee, thank you.' From the stage, one tends to assume that the friendly smiling faces out front belong exclusively to innocent, un-committed victims of the struggle—there's no way of guessing how many of those who clap and stomp to 'When You're Smiling' or 'Love is Just Around the Corner' will go out into the night to plot and conspire or even take up arms themselves. The most we can say for our foolhardiness is that they don't actually fight while we're playing.

The concert ends early, as in Beirut, so only about four-and-a-half hours have elapsed since we rose, heaving and grunting, from Albert's table, and here we are assembling outside the cinema to be ferried to a nearby steakhouse for another meal. I go with an English schoolteacher called Paul whose Lebanese brother-in-law owns the Cheyenne Restaurant. Paul, who has helped to organize our concert, walks with a limp, having picked up a stray bullet in the leg during the fighting. It was he who told us this afternoon how narrow Roy's escape had been, and in the car he regales me, as if to emphasize the point, with a story of an Englishwoman, driving her husband home from a party, who failed to hear a sentry's order to halt and arrived home to find that her husband, slumped in the front seat, was not sleeping but dead, shot in the head.

The scene in the Cheyenne is far removed from such morbid experiences. The shiny wooden tables are packed and, behind the cheerful hubbub, an orchestra plays. Well, not exactly an orchestra but a piano and drums duo, amplified with heavy night-club echo. The drummer sings, having apparently learned the English song lyrics phonetically—and approxi-mately. In our honour, he does 'When the Sants Goes Matching Hin', and 'Fly Me to the Moon' produces the

surrealistic couplet 'Show me what the string is like ...
indubitably Mars'. While we wait, none too impatiently, for our
steaks, there are *crudités* to nibble and we note that Albert's
gourmet instincts prompt him to mix his own blend of HP
Sauce and tomato ketchup into which to dip the slices of raw
carrot and cucumber.

It's phoning home night tonight (I could write a book about
Places From Which I Have Tried—And Usually Failed—To
Phone Home), and twice during the meal I am taken, panting
and puffing, up a steep hill to the telephone exchange to try
and make contact with Barnet. In a small room designated
'International Calls', three or four members of the staff are
sitting in their vests playing cards and generating a thick fog of
cigarette smoke. Lines to London are engaged the first time,
and when I return much later, all the card-players bar one are
tucked up in camp beds. Having got through, I carry on a
long-distance conversation with Jill above their stentorian
snores.

Friday, 12 March 1982, Beit Mery
We don't have to leave for Beirut Airport until 3 o'clock this
afternoon, thus enabling the hospitable and expansive Albert
Rizk to issue another invitation for lunch at the Tivoli at
12.30. Forewarned, we skip breakfast and set off in various
directions for a brisk morning walk. My route takes me, on a
tip-off from someone at the hotel, to some magnificent
Roman ruins about half a mile up the hill behind the hotel—
quite substantial remains of a Roman temple and baths and the
foundations of a later Byzantine temple with unimpaired
mosaic floor. I snap away busily with my battered old
Konika—the juxtaposition of Roman pillars, umbrella-shaped
stone pines, a Mediterranean blue sky and distant snow-
capped mountains should come out well. I bought the camera
about twenty years ago at Wallace Heaton's, second-hand for,
I think, £39, and I've never learnt to do more than leave it at
the same settings and bang away on automatic, but I've got
albums full of good pictures. When it comes to the niceties, I
rather agree with blues singer Big Joe Turner who, when
shown a self-loading, self-winding, self-focusing camera with

158

automatic light setting, hurried out of the shop saying, 'Man, you've gotta go to *school* to work a thing like that.'

It's another enormous lunch with Albert, who is clearly a magnificent survivor. To hear him talk of the splendid food and wine available in Lebanon in general and his own restaurants in particular (he has another in the heart of Beirut), you would not even suspect that the country has just suffered a destructive civil war and is poised precariously on the brink of another. At one point he sweeps away all conflicting considerations with the ripe pronouncement, 'There's no doubt about it—food is one of the pillars of *joie de vivre*—it's true, why talk about it?' With which he scoops up a dollop of hoummous with a shovel of pitta bread and engulfs it. Before the end of the meal he presents me with a cookery book—*A Gourmet's Delight: Selected Recipes from the Haute Cuisine of the Arab World* by Aida Karaoglan—which he says contains several recipes from the chefs of his Al-Barmaki Restaurant in Beirut. He inscribes it 'To Humphrey. A Fine Gourmet'. His card reveals that he is President of the Federation of Tourist Syndicates of Lebanon. A great man—may he long survive.

We drag ourselves away at 3 p.m. to go to the airport for a 7 o'clock flight. I'm all for avoiding a last-minute rush, but four hours does seem a bit excessive. We get there in well under an hour and sit around for a further hour before Farquar arrives to see us through Customs. Between us all, we've taken in enough garlic at Albert's to get the plane off the ground unaided. I notice, glancing through my new cookery book, that many of the recipes take in garlic by the bulb rather than a clove at a time. Splendid but antisocial. We also discover to our delight a dish called Al-Barmaki's Tribal Fatteh, a description which seems to sum up Albert Rizk, mammoth doyen of Lebanese restaurateurs.

After a flight of an hour and twenty minutes, we arrive at Amman, met by a racy-looking young man in cap, scarf and tweeds who introduces himself as Martin Savage of the British Council. Like the Cairo people earlier this year, he is taken by surprise by the size of the bass coffin and flight box, which won't go into the transport he has organized. Sian, who telexed the exact measurements far and wide before we left London, gnashes her teeth prodigiously, but Martin's res-

159

ponse—'Not to panic, we'll sort it out'—goes with the cap and scarf. One of the ingredients of a long and happy life as a touring musician is the ability to persuade oneself that sitting stranded in a foreign airport at the end of a long day is, in Arthur Marshall's immortal phrase, all part of life's rich pageant. (As his heroically resilient schoolmistress once said to a wilting pupil, 'We're molecules, dear, hurled huggah-muggah into life's foaming crucible!') Anyway, it's not long before Martin comes back with two taxis with roof-racks, which are loaded up and follow us top-heavily to the Tiche ('Tikey') Hotel.

Once checked in, Sian, Martin and I gather for a brief conference about our itinerary. Apart from full-blown concerts in Aqaba and Amman, our contract here involves several days of filming for Jordanian television—some kind of documentary in which we shall be shown sightseeing and performing in sundry places of historic interest. The plan, when first mooted, was generally popular all round, since the venues comprised the Roman amphitheatre in Amman, the Roman remains at Jerash (around which we pranced at midnight on the '79 tour) and, above all, the Lost City of Petra which we were all set on seeing this time. Now it transpires that the lady producer and instigator of the documentary has gone off to Germany for some pressing reasons of her own, and her bosses and Martin between them have taken the opportunity to scotch the whole idea, with which they were less than enchanted in the first place. In short, the filming is off, but we shall still be taken sightseeing. At school, the announcement of an unexpected two-and-a-half days' holiday would have been the cue for whooping and capering but, I think to Martin's surprise, we all feel rather deflated. After Lebanon we're all primed for action and I was looking forward to our being the first jazz band to shiver the crumbling pillars and pediments of Petra with an alfresco blast. There's something sloppy and untidy about the alacrity with which the whole thing's been abandoned that smacks of intrigue, about which I don't wish to know.

Saturday, 13 March 1982, Amman
Buffet breakfast, then off on our sightseeing tour at 10.30,
visiting the Roman amphitheatre first. A Palestinian guide in
red-check duster head-dress takes us round, keeping us on the
move with the reiterated injunction, 'Come along, English.'
His accent has an American tinge but with touches of the
jaunty Cockney that Arabs inherited from British soldiers. I
have a weak bump of history, and the stream of Biblical facts
flows over me. The atmosphere is staggering, though, and I am
more than ever sorry that we won't have a chance to test the
open-air acoustics of the deep, bowl-shaped auditorium. I
wasn't aware that many of these Roman theatres doubled as
swimming-baths, with quite sophisticated devices for sealing
and flooding the orchestra stalls. John Barnes comes up with
the information, imparted to him somewhere along the way,
that this is the origin of the word amphitheatre, the prefix
amphi- being used, as in amphibious, to mean dual purpose or
'in two ways'. It sounds convincing, but I'll need confirmation
from the O.E.D. before buying that one. Our guide unveils
somewhat dubious history as he shows us the exhibits of
clothing, artefacts and historic tapestries and paintings in the
museum in one of the theatre's antechambers. 'David see
Ba'sheba take bath, she take off all clothes, then we know
David lost husband of Ba'Sheba.' Later . . . 'Pinch-us Pilate
wash hands, say, "I don't know nuffink about Jesus".'

From the amphitheatre we go to the Capitol overlooking
the city—a fantastic bird's-eye view of the seven hills with
buildings large and small forming a thick crust over all of them.
The amphitheatre in the middle seems to offer the only bit of
open space in the whole panorama. We meet two young
English ladies up here—an archaeologist called Jill who
introduces her sister by the Agatha Christie-ish name of Selena
Colchester. The former is useful as a guide through the
archaeological museum and the surrounding remains. Unfortunately they are accompanied by two barking, barging dogs
who are less welcome.

At last night's hotel briefing, Martin told us that we are
invited to an early evening party tonight, but that we needn't
go. He isn't yet tuned into our mood, which is to pick up on
anything and everything that's going on. When we get to the

161

party, it's not immediately apparent to us why we are on the guest list, since it seems to be a private get-together of archaeologists. Never mind—we are adept party conversationalists by this time and it may well be that the archaeologists are happy to have some living curiosities to examine.

Sunday, 14 March 1982, Amman
Set off in the minibus at 10.30 to drive to Jerash for today's sightseeing. Things are different now from our nocturnal visit two years ago when we wandered at will among the Roman remains. There is now a big car-park and reception building at the entrance, and we are stopped by a guide dressed like a policeman (or maybe vice versa) who tells the driver where to park and then marshals us all behind him for a guided tour. As if impelled to assert our British independence, we decide that after the journey we need a cup of tea first so we make him wait while we stream off to the rest-house. It turns out to be a good move, because while we sip our tea we spot Jill, Selena and their rampaging dogs careering over the site and eventually heading for their car. It's not that we spurn the human company, but we had enough of those bloody dogs yesterday.

When we are ready to start our police guide, who introduces himself as Akhram, falls us in like a military platoon and marches us off, spouting his well-prepared patter. A smooth, unblemished hillside once completely covered this sprawling city of pillars, colonnades, temples and theatres. Detective work by sundry historians and archaeologists unearthed the first remains in the early nineteenth century and the excavation was speeded up at the start of this century by the English archaeologist Lancaster Harding, whose name is much revered here. After we've taken in the forum and climbed, defying vertigo, to the top of the eggshell rim of the huge amphitheatre, we encounter a group of 'guards' (more accurately, site caretakers) relaxing in the sun on the hill slope above the ruins. Akhram hails them, introduces us to them as 'Harding's family' and negotiates on our behalf an invitation to join them for tea. So there we sit on the grass, sipping strong, black, honey-sweetened tea out of a very unethnic blue enamel teapot, while the guards and Akhram converse in guttural

Arabic amidst a spectacular display of gold teeth. We add our fourpennyworth in primitive sign language—Roy holds up the teapot to be photographed as an archaeological treasure and they all cackle gleefully.

All the way round, Akhram imparts information on an endless conveyor belt of grammatically eccentric English, commanding our attention like a conscientious sergeant instructor. It's all pretty indigestible to me, though he comes up with one or two diverting party tricks. While we perch dizzily on the rim of the amphitheatre, he stays below and demonstrates its acoustics by dropping a small coin in the centre of the floor, with a crash that resounds around the shell. We wait until it has died away, then call down 'Go on, Akhram, drop it then!', an indiscipline which earns us a stern but twinkling glance when we get down. Elsewhere en route he shows us a column, the sections of which are so finely balanced on top of each other that they tilt in the breeze. He demonstrates by inserting a sliver of cigarette pack in one of the cracks—at the first gentle puff of wind it drops out. The column has teetered like that for decades. He points out places where huge statues once stood, 'But religious people came in and smash them up—I think religious people are always the same, yes?'

I've done little justice to the magnificent ruins, but this is no travelogue and the visual experience won't translate into words. It occurs to me on the way round that our attitude to ancient relics can come dangerously close to that of those Luddites among record collectors who believe that old '78s' lose something when electronically remastered and transferred to a less scratchy LP. We are, after all, looking at the vestigial remains of covered streets and ornate buildings. If we let ourselves become too overwhelmed and enchanted by the sight of them, doesn't the implication creep in that they would lose their 'atmosphere' and magic if, by some miracle of science, they could be completely restored? Could whole buildings possibly be more staggeringly beautiful than these skeletal bones gleaming against the blue sky?

At the end of the tour, Akhram takes his leave with: 'I hope you are enjoyed with me.' We certainly are—with his smart green uniform and clear-eyed military look he has exuded an air of integrity that's reassuring in the mercenary field of tourism. When we tell him that we are off to Petra tomorrow, he gives us the names of two guides, reliable friends of his, whom we should look out for. When he's gone, we go back to the rest-room for a snack—there are some interesting birds to spot here. Out on the site, we saw black-eared wheatears, and there are yellow-vented bul-buls in the eucalyptus trees round the rest-house to add a nice ornithological bonus to a great day.

Back in the hotel, totally whacked, I look forward to an early night after our communal meal in the restaurant. A message arrives to say that Victoria, the errant TV producer, has arrived back and wants to see me, so I go and wait for her in the foyer. When she arrives, I recognize her as having been involved, in a subordinate capacity, in the disastrous televising of our 1979 Amman concert. She is a raven-haired, sultry-looking lady made up, with black-rimmed eyes and vermilion lipstick, as if for a silent movie. It's a face made for smouldering—and when she asks how the filming has gone and I tell her that it hasn't, she smoulders prodigiously on the settee opposite me. Eventually she finds words. 'Cancelled? How cancelled? I left full instructions . . . I do not understand what is going on!' Nor do I, I can tell her in all honesty, hoping that Martin Savage will turn up to take over. He does quite soon, but his somewhat casual explanation only stokes the flames. They are, frankly, at loggerheads—he is still all for abandoning the whole silly idea, she is dead set on salvaging something from the wreckage of her plans. She goes off to telephone her office and I have to sit up long past my planned early bed-time watching her pacing gloweringly up and down outside the phone kiosk as she waits for response from them. I have told Martin that, if she wishes, I'm quite amenable to go along with what is left of the original itinerary. Eventually she comes across to ask, 'What time do you leave in the morning for Petra?' When we answer 'Seven o'clock' she says, 'I will be there with my camera crew—all is arranged.' Relieved to have turned aside a tempest, I totter off to bed.

Monday, 15 March 1982, Amman
We assemble blearily at 7 a.m. Neither Victoria nor her camera crew are to be seen so, not to be done out of our day at Petra, we wait just a short time and then drive off, assuming that they'll make their own way. There's a newly-opened desert road that cuts the journey somewhat, and we set off along it in two taxis. The Arab philosophy of 'inshalah'—'if Allah wishes'—which so frustrates Westerners trying to plan for the future, becomes positively hair-raising when applied to over-taking or negotiating blind corners. Several times we seem to be on the point of head-on collision with a tanker or juggernaut. Fortunately, Allah is today disposed to spare us, and we get to Petra intact. At a high point in the road near our destination, we stop at a solitary shop by the roadside. A notice alongside it reads: WELCOME TO PETRA SOUVENIR SHOP. FROM THIS POINT YOU HAVE A GOOD VIEW OF PETRA MOUNTAINS. NICE PICTURES CAN BE BOUGHT HERE, ALSO FILM, SLIDES AND OTHER ACCESSORIES. We duly peer through our binoculars at the mountains, but Petra did not remain a lost city for centuries by showing off to the outside world, and we see little other than a craggy outline, so we press on impatiently.

At the head of the ravine that leads to the city, there's a clutch of buildings—a big terminus where tickets can be bought for the hire of horses, and a restaurant with balconies overlooking the scene. The whole area is teeming with American coach parties who are 'doing' Petra this morning and going on to the Gulf of Aqaba this afternoon. Overheard in the queue for the ladies' loo: 'What are we gonna see this morning?' 'Oh, I don't know—I think some old rocks and caves and things . . .' A young guide steps forward to take charge of us—no one can remember the names of the two guides recommended to us by Akhram in Jerash, so somewhat naïvely we ask him if he is acquainted with Akhram. The answer rebounds with the speed of a squash ball. 'Of course—he is my brother!' Bearing in mind that all Muslims are brothers in the sight of Allah, he is not telling an outright lie, but he would clearly like us to believe that the All-Provident One has directed us straight to the one man whom Akhram would recommend above all. He introduces himself as Ahmed.

We hire him anyway and he goes off to buy our tickets for seven horses—Bruce's response to the offer of a mount is, 'Sooner have a tooth pulled', so he will walk the three kilometres through the ravine to Petra itself. Our guide returns with the tickets, but says there is an hour's wait. When we vote to get our money back and walk, horses suddenly materialize—docile, broad-backed animals saddled with blankets and with an Arab groom in charge. I haven't been on a horse since 1931 and regarded it as dangerous and foolhardy then. Under pressure of my 15½ stone, my animal embarks on a 'go slow' strike, picking its way among the boulders with infuriating precision, its head drooping stubbornly. The Arab groom hands over to a small boy of ten who, armed with a switch from a tree, periodically galvanizes the animal into a craggy trot that seriously endangers my manhood. The others seem to have compliant beasts that keep going at a steady pace, although they seem to be doing no more than me, which is to sit inertly like a bag of sprouts with the reins dangling. We make an odd cavalcade, with Lord de Vere looking positively Wellingtonian in the saddle, Mike Paxton, with his long hair, Zapata moustache and coat-hanger shoulders looking like some ancient Scottish war-lord leading his men in a spot of marauding, and Grosser startling his horse every few yards with stentorian cries of 'wh-a-a-at?' We set off in a long procession down the narrowing ravine, a noisy column with the guards holding long-distance conversations in a cackle of throaty aspirates and rasping vowels and the Americans providing a descant of pointless enquiries. Behind me, a black lady quizzes her guide relentlessly, getting non-committal grunts in response. 'Are you married? . . . Do you have children? . . . How many children do you have? . . . Do you enjoy your work? . . . Is this your horse? . . . Do you have to wash it down every day? . . .'

The surroundings grow more and more fantastic as we descend. The track narrows to no more than fifteen or twenty feet, with the towering sandstone walls acquiring ever more weird patterns and conformations in psychedelic yellows, reds and oranges. As we near the bottom, Greco-Roman porticoes carved around cave mouths high in the walls give a hint of wonders to come.

Every brochure and travel book on Jordan contains a photograph of the entrance to the city, the narrow gash of light at the end of the ravine through which a sunlit segment of bright terracotta façade can be glimpsed. Even so, the sight makes one gasp with surprise. Across an open space, carved into the side of a sheer red cliff, is the intricate frontage of a Roman temple, complete in every detail—pillars, Corinthian capitals, embossed pediment and all. As we dismount and stand gaping, a contralto American voice, planking like a banjo, exclaims 'Is that IT?'

Ahmed, a smooth and handsome young man, gathers us round him and embarks on a word-perfect historical lecture that rattles on for ten minutes without a breath, ending with 'Was that OK?' He explains that he has recently spent three years at Jordan University, studying archaeology. I notice he refers throughout to 'minuments' for monuments. We've already had Pinch-us Pilate from the guide in Amman. Transposing 'o's and 'i's seems a failing that Arabs share with bad typists! From the gabble we take in that it was the nomadic tribe of Nabataea, around two thousand years ago, who settled in the secluded and protected gorge and, having acquired in their travels detailed knowledge of Greco-Roman architecture, applied it with incredible accuracy to the carving of magnificent façades for their public buildings and tombs. 'Buildings' is perhaps the wrong word, since the Treasury of Pharaoh, for example, whose entrance first confronts the visitor, is a chamber about the size of Hampstead Town Hall excavated out of the rock. The façade likewise is sculpted, the columns, on close inspection, showing no seams or joins. Considering the softness of the stone, it's amazing that the detailed carving has survived for two thousand years with so little erosion from the elements.

The American coach parties, after a quick lecture from their guides and a photo session in front of the Treasury, remount and depart noisily back up the ravine, so we are left with the place virtually to ourselves except for the Bedouin entrepreneurs who swarm around trying to sell us priceless relics that have been excavated that very morning. One of them chases me at a run all over the rock face—we must have looked like two mountain goats at courtship—waving fistfuls of

beads. There's no escape, so I end up haggling over a Bedouin necklace of orange beads that look like suppositories and feel like plastic to me. I beat him down from the equivalent of fifteen pounds to five, which I look on more as a modest ransom for my escape than an exorbitant price for junk.

At one point some of the guys vanish into a 'museum' in a cellar, Mick Pyne remembering to keep his Sony cassette-recorder running. The young man in charge, while acknowledging that some of the artefacts are new, claims that some are old and have been excavated recently. Some are what he calls Roman pornographic oil-lamps, embossed with the figures of 'woman and man making love'. Mick emerges asking, 'Is it a con or isn't it?' After a while you're past caring. Outside a small boy who has demanded a ludicrous price for some bauble turns the tables by offering Mick one dinar for his Sony.

After a couple of hours' leisurely exploration, it's time to get back to base for lunch in the restaurant. The return journey is no more comfortable. The small boy leading my horse has sussed that I am not keen on trotting and takes malicious delight in wielding the switch and goading the animal on into jolting animation. Our guide has told us that a quite lavish tip is *de rigueur* at the end—no doubt the Americans have inflated the going rate. A kick in the teeth would be a more just reward for my little horror, but I hand over cash with astonishingly good grace. As we walk up to the restaurant, there is a cry of 'Yoo hoo!' from the balcony. It is Victoria, announcing that she has arrived. 'Bad luck!' we cry in unison. 'You've missed it all!'

I have flattered the eating-place by calling it a restaurant— it's just a bare room with rows of trestle tables, like a transport 'caff', and the most promising thing on the menu turns out to be mince with loads of boiled rice that tastes like tapioca. While we eat, Victoria sits next to me rolling her eyes in a series of theatrical expressions ranging from entreaty to despair. She is trying to get us to go back down the ravine and go through the sightseeing all over again, for the benefit of her tardy cameras. I am holding out well until she pulls a fast one, intercepting all the bills on the way to the table and paying them behind our backs. Who was it who defined 'putting an ob' on someone as one of the essential ploys in the art of life?

An 'ob' is short for an obligation, and Victoria has effectively planted one on us while our guard was down. By way of compromise, I suggest that, since the Nabataeans forgot to carve a grand piano out of the rock and there is no easy way of getting bass and drums down the ravine, the front line—i.e. myself, Bruce Turner, John Barnes and Roy Williams—should pop down again for some quick filming. Immediately, the creative producer in her surfaces and she launches us into a scenario. First, it's up to the reception area to film us buying, and being draped in, Arab headgear. Meanwhile, she commandeers four horses to take us down the ravine again. By this time, the regular old plodders have been put out to graze since the Americans have all gone on to Aqabar this afternoon and the tourist rush is over. So it's a matter of bribing horsemen who are galloping up and down the ravine to hand over their mounts for an hour. The animal I get belongs to a boy in his early teens who was last seen careering over the rocks like the Lone Ranger in a chase scene. Up to this moment I always thought that smoke coming out of the equine nostrils was no more than an artist's device to denote power and a fiery temperament.

Victoria is already in a state of incipient panic over the light, so there's no time to look around for something more docile. I am hoisted into a saddle that has been polished as slippery as ice and has stirrups so short that I immediately adopt the Lester Piggott position. Dimly-remembered instructions about gripping with the knees are useless, as my knees are up by my ears. As Victoria and her cameras lead off in their truck, she screeches at us to follow and to act as if we were taking in the wonders for the first time. My horse doesn't walk, it tap dances, and the only way to stay on is to hang on grimly to the front of the saddle. When I start to act, I become aware that my face is locked in a rictus of sheer terror. And as we come to the first carved façades up in the cliff sides, Victoria's imagination runs riot. 'Sing something!' she cries. 'Sing some jazz as you look at the caves!' No activity has yet been devised that John Barnes won't fling himself into with enthusiasm, so he starts scat singing—'Zazu zazu zey, ba ba rebop . . .'—his beard jutting skywards. We all follow suit, boop-a-dooping up at the cliffside like raving madmen. A trick rider in a circus would find it a difficult routine to squat on top of a tap-dancing horse while at the same time scat singing towards the heavens, and I am suddenly overtaken by a pulsating rush of anger to the head. Sliding to the ground, I stomp across to Victoria in her truck, shouting, 'This is bloody ridiculous—I'm not breaking my neck for you or your bloody film!' She is visibly impressed and I get a lift to the bottom while she continues to film the others. It's only now that I get a chance to take in the sight of Bruce Turner on horseback, a startling tribute to Victoria's powers of persuasion. As he comes close, I ask, 'How you doing, Bruce?' 'Some fun, I'd say,' he answers without conviction. Once we're down in front of the Treasury and on terra firma, I spot my horse, which has been brought on down by its owner. Glaring balefully at its rear end with my foot twitching compulsively, I realize that it's a stallion. Wait till I tell my equestrian wife and daughter that I've ridden down a rocky ravine in Petra on a gassy and impetuous stallion!

For the rest of the filming, Victoria has a notion to shoot us one by one looking into camera and uttering philosophical thoughts about the surroundings and their effect on our musical susceptibilities. With light fading, there's only time to do John this afternoon, sitting on the steps outside the Treasury of Pharaoh playing the soprano sax and breaking off to say, 'Whenever I play, it comes from the heart—but this beautiful place inspires me to play with even more conviction.' Then we hurry on to the open theatre, where she has us perched like statues on four widely-spaced plinths, playing 'Big Butter and Egg Man' to the amazement of the Bedouin cave-squatters who appear like gannets on the overlooking cliffs. It's here that John acquires a new nickname. (Till now he has answered to Barnesy, J.B. and Boko.) From the well of the theatre, Victoria keeps yelling instructions to 'Rossi', and it dawns on us that she is addressing J.B. The rest of us fall in with it at once—'Come on, Rossi, move to your right . . . Rossi, Victoria's talking to you . . .'—and by the end of the afternoon it's well established. How she came to 'Rossi' is a mystery—she must have heard me calling him 'Barnsey' and got it wrong. But Rossi he will now remain.

Eventually we extricate ourselves and return to the top to continue our journey on to Aqaba.

It's late and quite dark when we check in at the Alkazar Hotel. Since Lebanon, our gastronomic fortunes seem to have taken a dive. The late supper for which we all troop into the dining-room consists of very tough braised beef and horribly sweet carrots, followed by rice pudding. We are somewhat relieved that Victoria is staying elsewhere, but before our meal is over, she arrives full of plans for the filming tomorrow. It seems that she has arranged for us to go in the morning to a local music shop were we shall be filmed enjoying a jam session with some local musicians. We shall then go to the beach for some fanciful shots which will include Roy Williams playing the trombone up to his neck in the briny. At this point, supported by Martin Savage, with whom we have restored contact, I put my foot down. With a concert in the evening we are not going to spend all day doing silly things for her cameras. We shall go to the beach to relax, and she can come along and get what shots she can, but there will be no acting.

Tuesday, 16 March 1982, Aqaba

We have arranged that Victoria will be at the beach at 10 a.m., and she has until noon to do her filming, after which we shall have the day to ourselves. True to form, she arrives with her camera crew at 11.30. By now she is wary of this highly-temperamental band leader, and for a while she keeps her distance, presumably photographing our leisurely activities through a telescopic lens. It's a beautifully sunny day. The view, looking one way across the gulf to Elat in Israel and the other, to the granite-grey mountains of Wadi Rum, is spectacular, and we are generally speaking in a mellow mood. So we eventually wander across, exchange morning greetings with Victoria, and volunteer to do some more interviews for her. We are in Lawrence of Arabia territory here, a fact which awakens the romantic instincts of both Dave and Mick. When it comes to their turn to sit on an upturned boat and soliloquize into the camera, they wax positively lyrical. 'The piano is the orchestra of the world,' intones Mick, to which Dave follows with: 'When I look out to sea and see the waves rising and falling, it reminds me of my instrument.' Up at the beach bar afterwards I ask Victoria to send me a video copy of the TV show when it's finished, a thought that spreads consternation. 'The piano is the orchestra of the world' may get by on some distant foreign TV show, but circulation among the London jazz fraternity is a different matter.

The concert this evening is in a bizarre but romantic setting—stage and chairs are set up in a well, open to the sky, in the centre of the hotel. We're overlooked on three sides by three storeys of balconies that run outside the hotel bedrooms, handy for anyone wanting to watch from above, not so good for anyone bent on retiring quietly for an early night. The audience is predominantly British, European and American, although the Governor of Aqaba and his 'cabinet' are in the front row. During the interval I am presented to him and we chat about Jordanian music. I manage to keep a perfectly straight face when he extolls the virtues of a Jordanian bazouki player seemingly called Jamal Arse. A heady show, very well received, which Victoria captures on film.

Wednesday, 17 March 1982, Aqaba
It would have been nice if the tour had ended yesterday, on a natural climax. Today we drive back to Amman and, after a final routine reception, do the last concert in the Palace of Culture. Dairy-wise the event was more fruitful on the 1979 trip, when the intervention of television threw the whole sound-system into chaos. This time everything went without a hitch, but the Palace of Culture is a huge place with little atmosphere and it was a low-key affair.

Thursday, 18 March 1982, Amman
At Amman Airport, the gremlin with the specific function of organizing crises has a final fling. When the baggage is weighed in, we are informed that there is an excess to pay amounting to the equivalent of £1,300. Before the start of the tour, the British Council took out excess baggage vouchers which, up to now, have more than covered our requirements. How has it suddenly leapt to a £1,300 shortfall? We ask for a senior clerk to check it, and he confirms the amount. We are now in a quandary since we can't embark until the excess is paid. Sian

173

Griffiths is no longer with us, having left early this morning to go on to Damascus. Anyway, it's unlikely that she would have been able to rustle up that kind of money. Martin Savage is here, but is only carrying a small float against minor accidents. He rings his office and speaks to his boss, who agrees to send someone out to the airport with an open cheque, while at the same time commenting somewhat acidly on the extravagance which has so boosted our travelling weight. While we are waiting for the messenger to arrive, Martin is summoned to the weigh-in desk, where they offer profuse apologies and confess that all along they have misread the vouchers—there is nothing to pay. So we are allowed on board the plane and head for home. Next stop, Chesham High School on Friday.

Wednesday, 7 March 1984, London

It's been a strange experience putting this journal together in the past few weeks. Barely two years have elapsed since the last of the events described, yet the onward charge of modern history has contrived to make them both topical and remote. When we were in Poland, the Solidarity Movement, if it existed at all, had not impinged upon public consciousness. Now it has been and, for the time being, gone, carried on a tide of events that have pushed the notion of a huge, free-wheeling international jazz festival in Warsaw into the realms of fantasy. I wonder how the easy-going, aristocratic Mark has fared in it all—his spell in prison indicated that he was up to something back in those days, but I can't think that his brand of dissidence had much in common with that of Lech Walesa.

Looking back on our tours as a whole in the light of subsequent history, they do seem to follow a rather unfortunate pattern. Not long after we played in Turkey, the country underwent an upheaval leading to military government. No sooner had we turned our backs on Damascus than Syria came so close to open conflict with Israel that for a while it closed its borders to foreign visitors. North Yemen had a short-lived uprising within weeks of our departure from Sana'a, and it was almost exactly a month after our appearance in Lebanon that civil war broke out again.

It makes it hard to follow the news bulletins dispassionately. When they say that the US Navy has bombarded positions in the mountains behind Beirut, one has to accept the possibility that Albert Rizc's lovely little Tivoli Restaurant at Brummana has been smashed to bits or the Roman ruins at Beit Mery laid waste. Almost nightly nowadays I scan the TV screen intently to see if I can spot, amidst scenes of devastation in West Beirut, the Duke of Wellington pub sign jutting defiantly outside Mr Mounir Sama'a's Mayflower Hotel. And what of the people themselves? In my diary I described Albert as a 'survivor', and I cling to a vision of him sitting at his groaning table extolling the civilizing virtues of food while bombs, shells and bullets of every denomination keep a respectful distance. A week or so ago, during the height of the conflict, I put in a long-distance call to Lebanon to try to find out how he and other friends were faring. Every Beirut number, not surprisingly, gave the engaged signal.

In the Gulf, the status quo has been maintained. Indeed, we have been back on a six-day tour for commercial promoters, working in Al Ain, Abu Dhabi and Dubai in the United Arab Emirates. On the day we landed, one of the wives of the ruler of Dubai died, initiating a seven day period of mourning. It's characteristic of the ambivalent aspect of life in Arabia, where nothing is what it seems, that we did contrive to fulfil all our engagements.

Nevertheless, tension has mounted since we were there, and it may well be that the notion of a jazz concert in Kuwait or Abu Dhabi will one day seem as outlandish as that of a six-day, all-comers festival in Warsaw. Be that as it may, as far as I am concerned Arabia has already cast its notorious spell. Say 'the Middle East' to me and I think, not of crisis and tension and fighting in the streets but of a Beirut that is beautiful, not because of the buildings now demolished, but because of the people; of Victor in Damascus, ensnaring a customer with 'Do us a fyvour, mush, I've got no bloody chance with you'; of the market people in Sana'a, treating with friendly indulgence a mad Englishman with a skirt on over his trousers; and, most of all, of the young people of Yarmouk University, eager to cheer to the rooftops seven total strangers playing an alien music that offered not even a snatch of Beethoven to hang on to. I don't understand it, but I love it.